Hospice without Walls

HOSPICE WITHOUT WALLS

The Story of West Cumbria's Remarkable Hospice at Home Service

ANDREW BIBBY

Foreword by HRH The Prince of Wales
Preface by Margaret Forster
Photographs by Ski Harrison

CALOUSTE GULBENKIAN FOUNDATION, LONDON

Above: Miners' cottages at Pica, an old pit village between Whitehaven and Workington, with the Cumbrian Fells in the background.

Frontispiece: Loweswater, Cumbria.

Cover: A Macmillan nurse visits a Hospice patient at home.

Published by the
Calouste Gulbenkian Foundation
United Kingdom Branch
98 Portland Place
London WIN 4ET
Tel: 0171 636 5313

ISBN 0 903319 86 1

British Library Cataloguing-in-Publication Data. A catalogue record for this book is
available from the British Library.

Designed by Chris Hyde
Printed by Expression Printers Ltd, IP23 8HH

Distributed by Turnaround Publisher Services Ltd, Unit 3, Olympia Trading Estate,
Coburg Road, Wood Green, London N22 6TZ. Tel: 0181 829 3000

CONTENTS

Author's Acknowledgment

I am extremely grateful to all those people involved in West Cumbria Hospice at Home who helped me in the researching of this book.

In recounting the story of the Hospice it is impossible to acknowledge everybody's contribution; some people will find that their names appear in the text, while others with an equal claim to be featured will not. Also, people are named here only with their permission. I hope, however, that all who have played a part in the development of West Cumbria Hospice at Home will take pleasure and pride in the collective achievement which this book records.

Andrew Bibby is a writer and journalist, whose work appears regularly in *The Observer*. His last book, *Teleworking: Thirteen Journeys to the Future of Work,* was also published by the Calouste Gulbenkian Foundation.

Margaret Forster was born and brought up in Carlisle and lives for a part of each year in West Cumbria, her most recent book, *Precious Lives* (1998), records the deaths, and lives, of her father and sister-in-law.

Ski Harrison lives and works in Devon. She concentrates mainly on documentary and informal portraiture, usually working in black and white. *Celebration of Age,* an exhibition of 15 years of photographing the older generation, was supported by the Gulbenkian Foundation in 1994.

The Hospice movement has helped to create, over many years and often with minimal resources, a compassionate, much cherished and truly human way of looking after the terminally ill which has won my constant admiration. The West Cumbria Hospice at Home, of which I am proud to be the Patron, has over the ten years of its existence pioneered an entirely new system of hospice care. It has no hospice building of its own but, working closely with the existing Health Services, it brings professional medical and nursing care to those who prefer to depart this life in their own homes. It has helped to ease greatly the burden on families who are caring for a sick relative. And it has helped to bring comfort, compassion, love and dignity to all those whom it has looked after during the last months of their lives.

The West Cumbria Hospice at Home represents to me an important step forward in the care of those who need so much of our help. I commend its example to everyone who will read this book.

Preface

I wish I didn't have personal experience of why a hospice at home service is so needed, but I do. Three years ago, when my sister-in-law was told she had terminal cancer, the first thing she said was, 'I want to die at home'. I was surprised. Her local hospice had looked after her so well during a course of painful radiotherapy and she had been so relieved to stay there. But apparently dying was a different matter. She didn't want to go into the hospice. She wanted to die at home, in her own bed, among her own things.

So we promised, her partner and I, that she would. I dreaded it. As the last weeks went on and the caring grew harder, I wished I hadn't promised. We had teams of nurses helping – Marie Curie nurses, Macmillan nurses, district nurses – all wonderful, but we didn't want teams. The strain, emotional and physical, was dreadful. We yearned for the unobtainable, for the security a hospice offered without my sister-in-law needing to go into it.

We wanted, in fact, exactly what the West Cumbria Hospice at Home service so brilliantly offers. It is, I am convinced, a model for the future, giving as it does both the dying and the carers confidence and support of the kind they need.

Margaret Forster

In the Midst of Life

Three-thirty in the morning. The pain wakens him with a jolt. The nurse gives him some pills. She arranges the pillows and eases the pressure off his tender shoulder. Before the pills have had time to act, her smile makes him feel better.

The familiar loop of thoughts − it isn't fair − no one promised life would be − had some good luck too − married the right woman − had the family they wanted so much − it will be hard for them − so weak and weary ... He thinks of his parents and his childhood. He remembers the fells he climbed and the becks he fished. Soon he is asleep.

His wife sleeps on in the next room. She has had so many disturbed nights in the last few months. Hard work, worry and lack of sleep have brought her to the limit of her strength. Now, with a nurse there at night, she gets the rest she needs to continue to care for him in their home.

They have known for months that he will die of the cancer. They have accepted the fact in a way that has surprised them both. They talk about it frankly. They have never felt so close in their lives. Every day is precious.

The GP calls frequently. He has explained what is happening and has told them to ring whenever they need him. The hospice consultant came when he had severe pain which the medication no longer helped. The cancer had spread into his bones. She arranged special X-ray treatment which rapidly stopped the pain.

Nurses they have known since the children were small call every day. There are other nurses. The Macmillan nurse has helped with practical advice. She always seems to have time to listen to their problems. Now he needs more care, a Hospice at Home nurse has been staying all night. Their home has become a hospice. He will stay there to the end.

Dr Brian Herd

INTRODUCTION

Andrew Bibby's portrait of the remarkable 'Hospice without Walls' or 'Home Hospice' pioneered in West Cumbria carries implications of wider lessons for all of us. Besides the direct benefit of enabling people to end their final days in dignity and a familiar setting that they prefer, the account of the successful efforts to achieve this shows how such good voluntary projects bring out the best in men and women, and can unite people from every walk of life even in scattered or far from privileged areas. Illness and dying are challenges none of us is likely to escape, and the support that hospices – like hospitals and the National Health Service – receive from all sections of society eloquently demonstrates the potential which is latent but achievable in a real community.

Now that sex is so freely discussed, death is perhaps the subject least readily mentioned in conversation today. George Soros has recently funded a project on death in America, following the personal experience of his father's death, stating: 'I think our whole society is somehow operating in a state of denial and distortion. We have been told all about sex, but very little about dying.' David Kessler in *The Rights of Dying* said that a dying person has the right to be treated as a living human being; to maintain and to be cared for by people with a sense of hopefulness, however changing its focus may be; to participate in decisions about his or her care and to express feelings about death in their own way; together with the right to die, not alone, and in peace and dignity. The Natural Death Centre argues for the right of a person dying to have 'sufficient support from the NHS and the community to die at home, if so wished, whether or not they have relatives to care for them', as well as the same expertise in pain relief as they would receive if occupying a hospital or hospice bed; and the right to have 'midwives for the dying or their equivalent' to attend to their physical, emotional and spiritual needs.

One of our hopes in commissioning and publishing this book is to encourage similar communal projects – as are now starting to happen – in other areas of the United Kingdom and Ireland, as well as elsewhere. Such instances of people coming together to make realisable the most civilised context in which an event, inevitable for us all, takes place, can express and help fulfil admirable human instincts which we risk having lost with the weakening of the extended family.

Ben Whitaker
Director, UK Branch, Calouste Gulbenkian Foundation

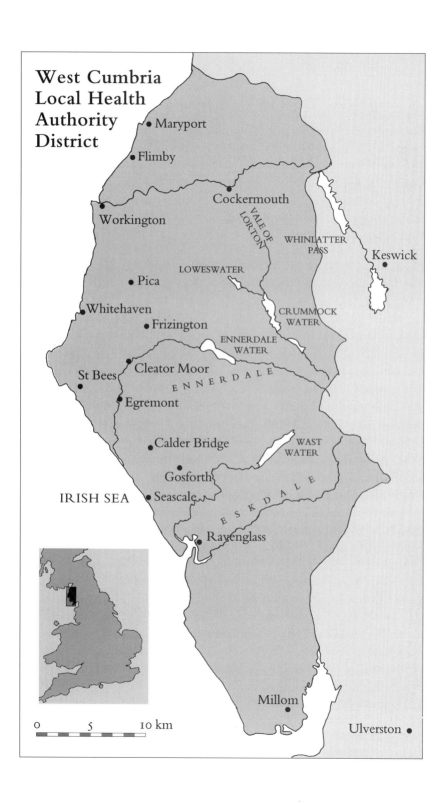

West Cumbria
Local Health
Authority
District

Maryport

Flimby

Cockermouth

VALE OF LORTON

WHINLATTER PASS

Keswick

Workington

LOWESWATER

Pica

Whitehaven

CRUMMOCK WATER

Frizington

ENNERDALE WATER

St Bees

Cleator Moor

ENNERDALE

Egremont

Calder Bridge

WAST WATER

Gosforth

Seascale

ESKDALE

IRISH SEA

Ravenglass

Millom

Ulverston

0   5   10 km

1 . The Hospice Movement

This is a book about a voluntary organisation, the work it does and the way in which it allows many different people in its community to contribute to its success.

The organisation is the West Cumbria Hospice at Home. Like other hospices up and down the country, it provides care for people who are dying. Like other hospices, its aim is to make the last days of life as dignified – as fully human – as possible. Like other hospices, it is concerned with meeting not only the medical needs, but also the social, emotional, psychological and spiritual needs of people who find themselves approaching the end of their lives.

As we shall see, however, the West Cumbria group has chosen a rather different way to undertake its work from that adopted by many other hospices, for it does not focus its work on a building. There is no 'hospice' as such to visit: instead, the organisation works almost entirely in the community, aiming to enable as many people as possible to stay in their own homes until the moment when death arrives. As its name makes clear, this is a 'hospice at home'.

West Cumbria Hospice at Home was established in 1987 and is part of a national hospice movement which, over the past quarter of a century, has seen an unprecedented growth of hospice provision in almost every city and town in Britain. Some hospices are run as NHS units but most are independent charities based in their own communities, managed by local people and dependent on the money donated locally for their continuing survival. The West Cumbria Hospice at Home is unusual in that it set out to meet the needs of the whole of a local health authority district (West Cumbria), rather than a particular town or part of a city.

According to the Hospice Information Service (based at St Christopher's Hospice, Sydenham) the total number of British hospices is now about 230, of which 151 are voluntary or independent initiatives. Because there is no one central hospice charity,[1] it is easy not to realise just how significant the hospice movement has become within the voluntary sector. For instance, the voluntary hospices' combined income – something over £150m a year – makes them collectively larger than any single fundraising charity, at least twice as large in income terms as well-known organisations such as the RNLI, Help the Aged or the Salvation Army.

The work of the hospice movement has been well documented, and this book will not attempt to repeat what others have said. However, it may be useful at this point to offer a brief history of the movement.

The hospice movement in Britain can be traced back to 1967, when St Christopher's Hospice was opened in Sydenham, south London, although its roots lie deeper. The use of the word 'hospice' (originally simply a place often run by religious orders where strangers received shelter or refuge) to refer to a house which cared specifically for dying people goes back to the nineteenth century; to the work, for example, of the Sisters of Mercy in Ireland and of the Sisters of St Margaret in Britain. The hospice founded by the Sisters of St Margaret in 1891 is still operating today as Trinity Hospice in Clapham. By the turn of the century two other hospices, St Joseph's and St Luke's Home for the Dying Poor, had been set up in London.

Nevertheless, St Christopher's is often described as the first modern hospice, a recognition of the pioneering role that it has played in helping to transform the way in which people suffering from terminal illnesses – especially cancer – are cared for. St Christopher's has also helped to pioneer new approaches to the care of the dying (in particular in the area of pain relief) which have stimulated the development of a new field of medical endeavour known as palliative medicine.

The inspiration behind the founding of St Christopher's, and still the hospice's leading light today, is Dame Cicely Saunders. Now over 80 years of age, she is both a medical doctor and a qualified nurse, as well as having additional social work qualifications. Characteristically, however, she declines to accept the tag of 'founder', preferring to put the credit elsewhere. Writing in 1998, she describes the origins of the hospice in this way:

When I first met David Tasma he was a Jew who had lost his faith, a Pole who had lost his homeland and a ghetto survivor who had lost friends, family and material possessions. At the age of 40 he was dying. In the months that followed, we talked again and again about how the passage to the end of life

---

1. Help the Hospices operates nationally in support of the local hospice network and publishes a *Directory of Hospice and Palliative Care Services in the United Kingdom and Republic of Ireland*. Its address, and that of the National Council for Hospice and Specialist Palliative Care Services are given on pages 90–1.

could be made easier and by the time he died, in February 1948, the idea for St Christopher's Hospice had been born. David was not just its founder but its first donor ... That was nearly 50 years ago, but ... we have never lost sight of the values that were so important to David: commitment to openness, openness to challenge and the absolute priority of patients' own views on what they need.

From the work of St Christopher's, and other early hospices such as St Luke's in Sheffield, has spread the network of local hospices across Britain.

West Cumbria Hospice at Home is a part of this movement. In its way of operation, however, it throws down something of a challenge to those who assume that the 'hospice as building' model is the only appropriate path to follow. As will become clear, the people who have launched and run West Cumbria Hospice at Home maintain that, because they have a hospice without walls, the service they can provide better meets the needs of their patients who live in the scattered towns and villages of a sparsely populated area. Arguably, it is also more in tune with fundamental hospice philosophy. Research shows that, given the choice, the overwhelming majority of people would prefer to die in their own beds in their own homes. A hospice service which concentrates on providing care at home can help make this possibility a reality for many more people.[2]

This book is primarily intended to explain how West Cumbria's 'hospice at home' model works in practice, but I hope the story will do more than this. It will demonstrate just how many people give their time to the work of this organisation, and how much they collectively contribute to its development. And in so doing, it will perhaps enable West Cumbria Hospice at Home to take on a wider, more representative, role, as an example of all the other community-based groups and organisations in Britain which are launched and develop through the commitment, hard work, enthusiasm and courage of their members.

---

2. There are other good examples of home hospices, for example the Hospice of the Marches, on the southern Welsh border, based on Tredegar, which was founded by Dr Richard Lamerton, who trained under Dame Cecily Saunders and who helped start the Macmillan nursing service.

2. NURSING IN THE HOME

THE NURSING SERVICE

West Cumbria Hospice at Home has no building, but it proudly claims to be able to provide almost all the services which a traditional in-patient hospice would offer. Home nursing is at the heart of its operation. Nursing was the service with which the Hospice began its work, only a few months after its founding meeting in 1987, and it remains the service for which it is best known. Home nursing takes the lion's share of the Hospice's budget – in 1997-8, about £170,000 out of total charitable expenditure of £290,000. Certainly, as far as the patients are concerned, the nurses *are* the Hospice. It is appropriate, therefore, to begin this account by looking at what their work involves.

This being Cumbria, it is possible to have misapprehensions about what a typical home visit is like. An isolated cottage high up on the fells, perhaps, where the shepherd and his family rely on spring water and make do without electricity ... The nurse who parks her car in the valley bottom, trudges her way up an indistinct farm track with light from a hand-held torch and the stars overhead ... The lights shining out across the hills from the cottage windows, as the patient is carefully tended through the night ...

Just occasionally, a West Cumbria Hospice at Home nurse may have this sort of experience. The area covered by the Hospice includes the western edge of the Lake District, with beautiful Wasdale, Eskdale, Ennerdale and the Vale of Lorton, and of course the Hospice undertakes to provide its home nursing service to all patients who need it, wherever they may happen to live. But, as we shall see, most of the population of West Cumbria live in the towns and villages along the coastal plain. In any case, stereotypes can be inaccurate: when the West Cumbria Hospice did provide nursing care recently to a patient living in an isolated cottage on the fells, a mile or so from the nearest house, the person was not a Cumbrian hillfarmer but a well-known broadcaster and writer.

Opposite: A Macmillan nurse visits a Hospice patient at home.

And while it is true that one of the Hospice's nurses once found herself snowed in at a patient's house (so that her one shift became a three-day session, staying in the patient's spare room), this happened in a small town on the coast during an exceptionally bad spell of winter weather, rather than high up in the hills.

For the nurse, the news that the Hospice needs them to look after a new patient will normally come in a telephone call, possibly at quite short notice. West Cumbria Hospice nurses generally do not have regular hours of working; instead, the Hospice has a bank of about 70 nurses which it has recruited and trained, and which it can call on as and when needed. Each nurse identifies every month in advance the shifts which they will be available to undertake. Some are more or less full-time with the Hospice; others work only on an occasional basis as a Hospice nurse, and may undertake additional part-time nursing work elsewhere.

The chances are that the phone call, from the tiny office in a health centre in Workington which serves as the Hospice's main administrative centre, will be offering the nurse a night shift. The Hospice sometimes provides a patient with daytime nursing care, and exceptionally may provide 24-hour care. It is much more common, however, for Hospice nurses to come in from 10.30 at night till 7.00 the next morning, to help patients and their families through the difficult hours of darkness. Among other things, this enables family members who are caring for a sick partner or relative to catch up on some sleep.

In 1997-8 (the Hospice year runs from April to March), West Cumbria Hospice at Home provided in total 1,813 nights of care as compared with 539 days. Night nursing care has increased slightly over recent years, while the level of daytime nursing has stayed more or less constant.

The nurse will be given the address of the patient's home and will make their own way there in time for the start of the shift. This can sometimes be a daunting prospect, especially if the area is not familiar. The nurses say that, when possible, they often make a brief call earlier in the day, partly to introduce themselves but primarily for their own benefit, to see what they can expect when they turn up again late in the evening to begin their shift.

THE EXPERIENCE OF NURSING IN THE HOME

'It is,' one Hospice nurse said, 'quite an honour to be accepted as a stranger into somebody's house.' It can also be challenging. People's personal circumstances can differ greatly, and their homes reflect these differences. Certainly, not every home will necessarily have the comfort and amenities of a purpose-built hospice. As the story told by another of the Hospice's nurses makes clear, it can be important to approach the job in a flexible frame of mind: 'In one place, there was absolutely nowhere to sit. The wife said, you'd better get into bed with him.' (Fortunately for all concerned the nurse managed to improvise an alternative.)

Then there may be the non-humans to cope with: 'Pets can be an absolute dread. There was the night when a snarling dog barred me from the kitchen. I had been warned not to enter the room but the trouble was, the spouse of the patient I was caring for became ill herself and took refuge in there. I was really thankful when the lady emerged – the snarling gnashers had been quite off-putting!'

Some encounters can be especially problematic. One nurse, caring for a mother with young children who was suffering from breast cancer but who was separated from her husband, was doing a night-shift session when the ex-husband turned up banging loudly on the front door, blind drunk. 'The wife told me that I'd better let him in, and he came and lay down on a couch. But I stayed on late the next morning, until I'd made sure that the children had been got off safely to school.' This sort of story is exceptional. Nevertheless the Hospice nurses have to prepare for long shifts, sometimes without opportunities for breaks, where there is no colleague close at hand for support and where the emphasis has to be very much on self-sufficiency.

Hospice nurses also have to work without the normal professional trappings of a hospital or hospice environment, which can help define the patient-nurse relationship. Sue Blakeney, who has been working more or less full-time for the Hospice for nine years, was previously a hospital theatre nurse and can contrast the two experiences: as she says, there is no professional 'barrier' for nurses to hide behind in the home. She adds quickly that she feels that this is the way it should be, but that she found the experience strange initially.

Another member of the Hospice nursing team is Gillian Bickersteth, who previously worked as a practice nurse in a GP centre in Carlisle. She too contrasts the two types of nursing experience, mentioning another area where the home Hospice nursing service has removed the usual professional trappings of nursing: 'There is a deliberate policy here of not wearing a uniform, and at first I found this quite difficult,' she says.

On the other hand, the Hospice nurses stress the satisfaction of being able to undertake one-to-one nursing, in contrast to the usual rush and routine of an acute hospital ward where it can be especially difficult to make proper time for the terminally ill patient. 'It is incredibly rewarding work. It's demanding, but there is a real sense of being able to help, even if only in a small way,' Gillian Bickersteth says.

The nursing work itself can be very varied. Some shifts, particularly night shifts where the patient is able to get some sleep, may be relatively undemanding. In this situation, the hospice nurse may try to help make the carer's job the next day a little easier by doing some of the household chores: they may do the washing-up, and have even been known to tackle a pile of ironing. Hospice nurses may also have to respond to emergencies of the non-medical kind: in one house, a nurse was caring for a patient when a water pipe burst and the rest of the shift was spent desperately trying to mop up the resulting flood.

On the other hand, nurses may equally find themselves undertaking long shifts of hands-on nursing. Caring for the physical needs of someone whose body has begun to fail them is extremely hard work. Patients may need moving, washing and feeding, and their beds may need changing. The Hospice nurses also have a key role to play in palliative care treatment, for example ensuring that painkilling drugs are administered on time.

Traditional hospices are concerned with more than the physical care of patients, and the West Cumbria Hospice at Home shares the same philosophy. The days before a person's death can be, and perhaps ideally should be, a time for reflection, for looking back and for preparing for the journey ahead. The Hospice nurses' role in listening and talking to patients is as much a part of their work as nursing care.

TAKING ON NEW PATIENTS

West Cumbria Hospice at Home works with patients who are in the final stages of an illness. This is most likely to mean that they have one form or another of cancer. In 1997-8 the Hospice cared at home for a total of 130 new patients, of whom 107 were suffering from cancer.

Some in-patient hospices have restrictions on the types of illness they can deal with. West Cumbria Hospice at Home has a clear policy of accepting any terminally ill patient whatever their disease, and over the 11 years it has been in operation its nursing service has cared for patients in the end stages of a wide range of non-malignant diseases. These have included motor neurone disease, AIDS, severe chronic obstructive airway disease, multiple organ failure, rheumatoid arthritis and several other conditions.

While it does not differentiate between diseases, West Cumbria Hospice at Home does have some criteria for its service provision. To receive the home nursing service, a patient and their carer (usually their partner or other family member) must want care to be given at home and agree that it is possible. There must be no *medical* reason why admission to hospital is necessary (the qualification is important: as we shall see, many people who are dying end up in hospital for non-medical reasons, often because the family member caring for them just cannot cope any longer).

The local GP and district nurse must also give their consent before the Hospice will take on a new patient. West Cumbria Hospice at Home sees itself as complementing the NHS primary health professionals in their work, rather than offering a separate or competing service. In fact, referrals for the Hospice normally come from GPs or district nurses, though the Hospice will accept referrals from any source – including the patients themselves or their families. In such a case, however, the approach is referred back to the patient's own GP for their agreement.

Sometimes Hospice nurses will be called in only for the last few days, or even the very last hours, of somebody's life. The nurses know that they may get last-minute phone calls cancelling arranged shifts, because the person they were due to care for has died in the meantime. In 1997, 60% of the West Cumbria Hospice at Home patients received help for two weeks or less, although some patients receive Hospice care for longer. West Cumbria Hospice at Home has a small number of patients who have received its help for over six months. There may be several reasons for this: sometimes the Hospice offers occasional respite care to look after someone who is at an earlier stage in the development of their illness. As a general guideline, the Hospice sees its work as being with those who can no longer be cured, but who can certainly be cared for.

HELPING THE CARERS

There is a second group of people for whom West Cumbria Hospice at Home nurses provide a valuable service – the carers. Much of the work of caring for people in the last year of their life is undertaken not by health professionals but by members of the patient's own family or their friends. National statistics show that about a third of cancer patients receive care from one close relative, while nearly half are looked after by two or three relatives, typically a spouse and an adult child.

Caring for a loved one as they enter the last stages of an illness is work which most people perform willingly, but that does not mean that the task is not difficult and stressful. Caring for anyone who is physically ill is hard work, but coping with the emotional issues raised when

Ennerdale Water, Cumbria: the area covered by the Hospice at Home includes the western edge of the Lake District, with Wasdale, Eskdale, Ennerdale and the Vale of Lorton.

someone who is close to you is approaching death can be extremely distressing. A national survey of people who had nursed family members or friends through a terminal illness found that more than half subsequently described the work as 'rewarding' and only one in ten found it a burden.[3] A large minority of the survey described the task as being rewarding and burdensome in equal measure. If illness is prolonged the carers themselves can be left physically and mentally run down. Anxiety and depression are common and many carers feel isolated, particularly after the death has occurred. Carers also need adequate information, for example about the nature of the patient's illness and how best to care for them.

Working in patients' own homes means that Hospice nurses have a direct insight into the experiences which carers are going through. 'You see amazing devotion in families,' said one of the nurses. But the work is far from easy: Hospice nurses also talk of the survival techniques they

---

3. Amanda Ramirez *et al.*, 'ABC of Palliative Care: The Carers', *British Medical Journal*, vol. 316 (17 January 1998).

have seen adopted by family members, ranging from obsessive cleaning of the house to an over-enthusiastic embrace of the whisky bottle.

Gillian Bickersteth says that it can be difficult if patients and carers are not being honest with each other about the illness. 'Each side may be wanting to protect the other. Each knows that the patient is dying, but neither will acknowledge it. A lot of people feel that if they do acknowledge it, everything will fall apart. But that seldom happens – generally, it strengthens things. Of course it's hard and painful, but it can be healthy as well,' she says.

Not every home is a happy one. One might prefer the last few weeks of a person's life to be a time for reconciliation, for clearing up old misunderstandings and putting an end to old squabbles. The West Cumbria Hospice at Home nurses themselves say that they sometimes feel the impulse to attempt reconciliations between partners, or – especially in larger families – to bring warring factions together. But believing that this can be achieved is often unrealistic. The Hospice nurses discuss during their training the limits to their role: as one said, it is not possible to sort out 30 years of family disagreements in three weeks.

THE APPROACH OF DEATH

While no-one knows the precise moment when death will come, the prognosis for someone who has a terminal illness is not in doubt. Does this make the work of being a Hospice nurse particularly gruelling or emotionally draining?

It certainly puts these nurses into the relatively small category of people who have regular contact with dying and death, in a society in which the subject is still largely taboo and where it is therefore harder to talk generally to friends and acquaintances about this aspect of their work. Sue Blakeney, for example, says that she finds it helpful that her best friend also happens to be a nurse with West Cumbria Hospice at Home. 'People outside nursing find it very hard, and I don't really discuss my work with them. It's hard anyway, because we are not allowed to discuss individual patients outside our work situation because of patient confidentiality,' she says. She adds that people often ask her if she finds her job morbid. 'I say, no, I find it very rewarding. I can't really see myself doing any other job now.'

Nevertheless, the nurses say that there can be pressures on their own families. There are the regular phone calls to cope with, when booked shifts have to be cancelled because a patient has already died. One of the Hospice nurses recalls: 'My little boy asked me once, "Mummy, do all

Whitehaven, on the Cumbrian coast, once an important coal mining town and port.

your patients die?" and I had to reply, "Yes, they do". He said, "Well I never want you to nurse me!"'

The hospice movement aims to make dying as painless and natural as possible, while allowing patients to approach their own death in their own individual way. 'People's last dying moments need not be a solemn occasion,' Sue Blakeney says. On the other hand, sometimes the experience is less happy. Partners, family members and friends left behind have to come to terms with what has happened. 'Some can be calm, but sometimes people can be angry, and they can take that anger out on you,' says another Hospice at Home nurse.

Inevitably, too, the experience is not the same if the person who is dying is young. 'For 70 or 80 year olds, you can put some meaning to it. For 30 year olds, perhaps who have got young families, and who are not ready to die at that age, it's different,' Sue Blakeney says. One of her colleagues adds: 'It puts things into perspective – it reminds you not to take life for granted.'

Caring for children with terminal illnesses can be particularly difficult and sad. In its 11 years of work, the West Cumbria Hospice at Home has cared for patients ranging from 18 months to 102 years of age.

Perhaps the last word in this chapter should be given to Gillian Bickersteth. 'All I can say is what a happy organisation West Cumbria Hospice at Home is. A lot of nursing has lost its vocational aspect. Hospice nursing hasn't. I think if you lose the vocational aspect, you lose something important.'

3. The Early Years

THE FIRST PUBLIC MEETING

West Cumbria Hospice at Home can trace its origins to a public meeting held in Whitehaven in January 1987, when the idea of a hospice for West Cumbria was first put to the people of the area for their response.

January is not the best time of the year to call a meeting, particularly in a part of the country where many people have to travel quite long distances to attend. Nevertheless, groundwork had been done to ensure that the event was as successful as possible. Letters had been sent out to a wide range of local organisations: Round Tables and Rotary Clubs received an invitation to send a representative. Women's Institutes were contacted. All the churches were notified. So too were all the GPs in the West Cumbrian area, and the managers of the local Health Authority. The list grew and grew: other community organisations received the same standard letter. 'We wrote to absolutely everybody we could think of,' said one of those involved.

The work paid off. The organisers had hoped that there might be a hundred in the audience. In the event, 350 people turned up. There was a great deal of enthusiasm for the idea of a local hospice, and at the end of the meeting 36 volunteers came forward, offering to get more actively involved.

Right from the start, however, there was an idea that West Cumbria needed not a traditional hospice building, equipped with in-patient beds, but something a little different.

THE GUIDING SPIRITS

Most successful community organisations are rooted in the enthusiasm and commitment of a handful of founder members. In the case of West Cumbria Hospice at Home, two individuals in particular should share much of the credit for the charity's development. They are Margaret

Dowling, who worked as a district nursing sister in West Cumbria for many years and later became the Hospice's first Nurse Manager, and Dr Brian Herd, who came to Cumbria as a GP in 1965 and was still working in practice in the Cockermouth area at the time of his retirement in 1993.

Brian Herd lives a little way outside the small market town of Cockermouth, on the road which runs past the first of the Lake District mountains and eventually takes travellers over the Whinlatter Pass into Keswick. Even after some years away from his GP surgery a visit to Cockermouth can mean slow progress, as former patients in this small community recognise him and stop to chat.

Retirement has given him the opportunity to pursue other avenues, especially his interest in amateur dramatics: he regularly treads the boards at the little theatre in Workington and recently took time away from Cumbria to participate in a month-long drama summer school arranged by RADA in London. It has not, however, meant that he has stopped his work for the Hospice, where he has always played a central role. Brian became Chairman of West Cumbria Hospice at Home when it was first constituted, and has been its Chairman ever since. 'I trained as a physicist and became interested in cancer treatment before I became a doctor,' he says. 'I found caring for the dying one of the most challenging parts of general practice, immensely demanding both professionally and emotionally. I went on a brilliant course in Oxford, which opened my eyes to how much could be done to help, even when cure was not possible.'

This was back in the mid-1980s. In 1986, Brian Herd applied for a six-month postgraduate study sabbatical from his practice in Cockermouth, to look into the subject in more depth. One of his first visits was to St Christopher's Hospice in Sydenham, south London, which has always been a leader in the hospice movement. He also worked at St Luke's Hospice in Sheffield and the Strathcarron Hospice in Scotland, and visited about 20 other hospices and similar units.

His period of study leave was coming to an end, at the very beginning of 1987, when he received an approach from Margaret Dowling. Margaret had heard of his interest and was contacting him to ask him to chair the Whitehaven public meeting. It was coincidental that, at the same time as Brian Herd was following up his own professional interest in better care for terminally ill patients, exactly the same thing was being mulled over by Margaret Dowling and her colleagues.

Margaret was born and brought up in Huddersfield and completed her general nurse training at the Royal Infirmary there, though she moved early in her career to Cumbria. She retired from nursing in the spring of 1998 but remains the West Cumbria Hospice at Home's Vice-Chairman and – like Brian Herd – is actively involved in its management. She has a warm, enthusiastic personality, combined with a nurse's efficiency.

Margaret had been District Nursing Sister in a GP practice in Egremont, one of the smaller centres in West Cumbria, for several years in the 1970s. In 1983 she took up a new position as the first Macmillan nurse in West Cumbria, thereby taking on a particular role in the care of patients with cancer.

The Macmillan nursing service in Britain was first set up in 1975, and is the result of a partnership between the NHS and a charity, Macmillan Cancer Relief. Macmillan Cancer Relief takes its name from its founder: in 1911 Douglas Macmillan, a young man in his late 20s, saw his father suffer a painful death from cancer and determined to establish a charity to help other sufferers. (The charity was initially known as the National Society for Cancer Relief and for a short time became the Cancer Relief Macmillan Fund.) New Macmillan nurse posts are funded for three years by the charity, after which the local NHS health authority takes over responsibility. Twenty years after the service was first pioneered, there are now over 1,500 Macmillan nurses in post in almost every part of the country.

Macmillan nurses are specialists in cancer care, with training which enables them to give expert information and advice on treatment and on ways to manage pain, to offer counselling support and also to help on more practical issues such as state benefit entitlements and financial matters. Their role is not, however, to give the extended practical nursing care which Hospice at Home nurses can provide. Their workload (which may involve visits to as many as eight patients a day) would in any case make this impossible. What they do offer the Hospice nurses is back-up support and teaching.

As West Cumbria's first Macmillan nurse, Margaret was ideally placed to take a leading role in the establishment of a local hospice. But she was not alone. Also actively involved was Felicity Watson, a native Cumbrian who after a successful nursing career in London and Lancashire had become a community nurse manager in the area, responsible for planning and developing the introduction of the Macmillan nursing service. Felicity was one of the speakers at the first Whitehaven meeting and has been active as a Trustee of the Hospice at Home ever since, more recently taking on a coordinating role on the fundraising side.

WHY HOSPICE AT HOME?

The 1970s and early 1980s had seen a massive development of the hospice movement, and in most parts of the country, by the mid-1980s, hospices were either already established or were in the process of being set up. Other areas of Cumbria were discussing their need for hospices: further south, in the Furness area, a group was coming together to develop what was later to open as the St Mary's Hospice in Ulverston. Further north, similar moves were under way in the Carlisle area, which was in due course to see the development of the Eden Valley Hospice.

West Cumbrian people also wanted to support a local hospice, and indeed some people had already offered money towards a new hospice project. This was the background to the public meeting in January 1987, which saw West Cumbria Hospice at Home launched on its way.

But why a Hospice at Home? There were perhaps three reasons why the people who set up that meeting were already looking towards an innovative home-based hospice service, rather than the more traditional in-patient model.

THE GEOGRAPHICAL AREA

The first is to do with the geographical nature of West Cumbria. Brian Herd explains: 'When you look at the traditional nursing-home sort of hospice, generally they're based on fairly large catchment areas. But there isn't one centre of population in West Cumbria: if we had gone for a building, it clearly wouldn't have met the needs of all the patients in the area. It would have been fine for people in the locality, but further away people would have had to struggle on and look after patients at home.'

West Cumbria Hospice at Home's region chiefly comprises the long coastal plain of the Cumbrian coast from Maryport to Millom, an extremity of England beyond the natural barrier of the Lake District mountains. As Brian Herd picturesquely puts it: 'We have the sea on one side, and the sheep on the other.'

It is a large and isolated area. Getting around usually means a long drive along slow roads or a tedious journey on one of the infrequent trains – the 50 miles or so between Maryport and Millom takes 90 minutes by train, for example.

It is not primarily a rural area, but rather an old industrial centre with many working-class towns and villages which came into existence

Opposite: Sheep being judged at the Eskdale show.

because of what was under the ground: the coal seams of the Cumberland coal fields and the iron ore deposits nearby. Both industries have now disappeared, and the local economy is in a rather delicate state of health. This has meant that in recent years West Cumbria has suffered from more than its share of unemployment. At the time of writing, for example, male unemployment in Workington and Whitehaven is about 15%, in Cleator Moor about 16% and in Maryport over 18% (the Cumbrian average rate is below 10%). Of the ten council wards in Cumbria with the highest levels of social disadvantage, four are in urban areas of West Cumbria.

There are three principal communities. Whitehaven has fine buildings (not all in the best state of repair) to reflect its proud past as an important coal mining town and port. The last of the pits closed in the 1980s, but the industry had been in decline for a generation before that. Now the town is looking again at its potentially attractive harbour area as a focus for tourism. Workington, further up the coast, also has a predominantly industrial past, once again based on the Cumberland coalfields. By contrast, Cockermouth (which despite its name is several miles inland) is a traditional market town, on the edge of the Lake District National Park and indeed able to attract a small share of the important Cumbrian tourist trade.

There are also the smaller towns, places like Cleator Moor and Frizington inland from Whitehaven, with rows of nineteenth-century terraced housing built to house the workers in the iron ore industry. Further south are the communities of Seascale and Egremont; the BNFL nuclear complex at Sellafield dominates the landscape. Up the coast from Workington is the small industrial town of Maryport.

This is the varied region which, as the instigators of the 1987 meeting realised, the new West Cumbria Hospice would have to service.

THE FINANCIAL IMPLICATIONS

There was a second reason to be cautious of following the traditional route towards a physical hospice building, and that was the financial task which would have faced the group.

West Cumbria is not particularly prosperous (the Government has recently designated it as one of Britain's poorest areas), and even with tremendous local goodwill the effort of fundraising either to create a purpose-built hospice or to adapt an existing building would have taken

Opposite: Whitehaven. The West Cumbrian coastal plain is not primarily a rural area but an old industrial centre with many working-class towns and villages.

a long time. During that period, the hospice would obviously have not been able to meet the needs of patients who became ill. Instead, West Cumbria Hospice at Home was able to progress very quickly to provide a basic home nursing service: the first patient received night care in September 1987, only about seven months after the initial public meeting.

By contrast, other hospices nearby were still at the fundraising stage: 'We met with the chairman and trustees of another hospice, and it was very interesting. We were already up and running: they were years down the line, and still not providing a service,' Felicity Watson recalls.

THE CASE FOR CARING FOR PATIENTS AT HOME

Important as these two reasons were, however, they were not the main stimulus behind the Hospice at Home idea. In fact, even before the organisation became established in 1987, most of the people directly involved were strongly attracted to the home-based hospice model. Brian Herd says:

The more we looked at it, the more we realised that home is where patients want to be, and where relatives want to care for them. There are exceptions of course, but as a generalisation carers have a desperate need to look after the patients in their own homes.

If you look at the reasons for hospital admissions, a lot of the reasons are what we would call social rather than medical – in other words, carers feel that they can no longer continue to give care, rather than the patient actually needing medical expertise of the kind that you would only get in hospital.

So it seemed that if we were to put more care into the home, and to build on what is already there, we could do a great deal. That was the sort of thing we devised.

There was already a model for West Cumbria Hospice at Home to follow. The Marie Curie nursing service offers cancer patients in the terminal stages of their illness exactly the sort of one-to-one nursing care that the Hospice at Home had in mind. Marie Curie nurses in West Cumbria (funded jointly by the Marie Curie Cancer Care charity and the local NHS Health Trust) had also been involved with Margaret Dowling and Felicity Watson in helping to set up the first Whitehaven public meeting.

West Cumbria Hospice at Home wanted to go a step beyond the Marie Curie service in two respects. Firstly, it wanted to ensure that there were much greater resources available for this service than the necessarily limited Marie Curie provision for the area. Secondly, it wanted to extend the service beyond cancer patients, to enable all patients with terminal illnesses to receive care. (For several years subsequently, the Marie Curie service ran as a complementary service in parallel with the Hospice at Home in West Cumbria; from 1998, however, Marie Curie nurses have ceased to undertake home nursing in the area, and instead are now providing hospital-based nursing for cancer patients.)

By the late 1980s the hospice movement nationally was also broadening its approach. The importance of offering home care had been widely recognised, and many existing hospices had built up home-care teams. The work these teams undertook varied from place to place, some aiming to provide an advisory rather than a nursing service for patients. The importance given to the home-care service also varied; it would probably be fair to say that the majority of hospices continued to put their work with in-patient hospice residents at the centre of their operation.

THE FIRST YEAR

It was fortunate that Brian Herd, Margaret Dowling, Felicity Watson and the others who came together to start the West Cumbrian Hospice shared a common belief in the importance of centring their own work on home care. But they needed to convince local people, who were going to be the ones undertaking the fundraising and who could see hospice buildings appearing in other parts of the country, that the way forward was not to focus on bricks and mortar. How do you get community support for the much more nebulous concept of a hospice at home?

The success of West Cumbria Hospice at Home suggests that the task was perhaps not as difficult as some might have predicted: local people took up the idea very quickly. In fact, after the initial January meeting, things began to happen very fast. Immediately after the meeting the organisers arranged to consult a local accountant, Michael Roberts, and a local solicitor, Mary Todd, so that by the time of a follow-up meeting in February work was already well under way in agreeing a trust deed, which would act as the new charity's constitution. The February meeting elected the Trustees, with Brian Herd voted in as Chairman and Margaret Dowling as Vice-Chairman. It also agreed a management structure, with a small Council and a somewhat larger Executive Committee, which the charity still uses today.

By April, the Hospice's application for registration as a charity had been accepted by the Charity Commission. Thereafter, the new organisation's officers could turn their attention to the important relationship which the Hospice service would have to develop with the local Health Authority.

This issue is not necessarily straightforward, and tensions between voluntary hospice organisations and health authorities and NHS trusts have in the past been a regrettable feature in some parts of the country. Brian Herd says that the Hospice now has a very good relationship with the NHS but admits that in the very early days in West Cumbria the NHS was cautious about the new service: 'Initially, we weren't welcomed by the NHS. We were asked not to set up a separate charity, but to put money into a NHS amenity fund,' he says.

But the new Hospice at Home was in a strong position, not least because fundraising had got off to an excellent start. A five-figure donation from a local supporter had been a great boost, and by the summer £30,000 was already in the bank. A meeting with the Health Authority in June gave the Hospice the green light to start the nursing service, initially on a three-year basis. The service was to begin in September, when a small number of nurses were recruited. The first patient was taken on almost immediately.

West Cumbria Hospice at Home received its formal launch at a second public meeting in Whitehaven, held in October (incidentally on the same evening that the infamous 1987 hurricane was ravaging southern England). By this stage the Hospice had found itself a President, Dowager Lady Egremont, who lives in the area in her home, Cockermouth Castle. Lady Egremont was well-qualified to take on the role, not least because of the experience she herself had had as a voluntary nurse in Vietnam and elsewhere in South-East Asia.

The meeting included a talk on the Hospice's work but was also an opportunity for further fundraising, with an auction of goods donated by local well-wishers.

DEVELOPING THE NURSING SERVICE

From the one initial patient in September 1987, the nursing service quickly grew, under the coordination of Margaret Dowling (Margaret in due course became Hospice Nurse Manager as well as continuing as a Macmillan nurse). In the first 12 months, the Hospice had almost 40 patients. By 1988-9, this had increased to 56, and by 1990-1 to around 90.

By this stage, the first NHS funding had begun to arrive, as part of a nationwide initiative by the Department of Health to support the voluntary hospice movement. The first grant of £23,500 enabled West Cumbria Hospice at Home to launch a day-centre service for patients and a drop-in facility in Whitehaven, Millom and Cockermouth.

However, in line with its aim of providing all the services which a traditional hospice would offer, West Cumbria Hospice at Home had its sights set on a more ambitious development. As Brian Herd told the audience at the Hospice's AGM in the spring of 1991: 'West Cumbria has applied for funds for a Medical Director. If we receive the grant, we will be able to appoint a specialist in palliative medicine to be available to advise the GP on the management of cases admitted to Hospice at Home. He or she would provide medical support for the nurses involved and would have an important educational role.'

Shortly after the AGM, the good news came through: the new grant application had been successful, and NHS funds would in future be available to Hospice at Home to pay for a part-time Medical Director. In 1992 the organisation was able to appoint Dr Eileen Palmer to the post (initially a two-year appointment). It has turned out to be an inspired choice.

4. THE MEDICAL SERVICE

THE HOSPICE AT HOME'S MEDICAL DIRECTOR

Eileen Palmer is an engaging and lively figure, very committed to her work and without any trace of the stand-offishness sometimes associated with consultants. She came to West Cumbria from Yorkshire, having previously been the first Medical Director at the Prince of Wales Hospice in Pontefract. This is a traditional hospice, taking in-patient residents. Before her time in Pontefract, she worked for seven years as a GP.

She is in a good position, therefore, to be able to compare the work of the Hospice at Home with the more conventional hospice model. It is quickly apparent that she is committed to the idea of caring for patients in their own homes wherever possible. 'I am convinced that the work we are doing is right, important and necessary,' she says.

Behind this is an event in her own family which she says was a very powerful experience for her. Shortly after she qualified as a doctor, her father died at home. The opportunity to be with his family was something which Eileen Palmer says was enormously satisfying both for him and for them all. She describes the time like this:

As soon as he knew he had terminal cancer, he wanted to get home. As soon as the family knew, we all unanimously wanted him home. Home was a flat above a shop.

Within a week or two, all five of his children were gathered from all parts of the UK. The day before he died, we held hands around his bed and sang to him. Friends and neighbours stopped by.

The GP called. Downstairs the shop was still trading. The ordinariness of it all was of indescribable, inestimable comfort.

Dad died in his own bed in his own bedroom. The specialness of that, the moments of intimacy it allowed, the sense of being involved in his care and the knowledge deep in all our hearts that being home mattered more to him than anything else – all these things stay with me 20 years later.

Opposite: Dr Eileen Palmer, Hospice Medical Director, discussing treament with a patient.

While working in Pontefract, Eileen Palmer had taken a keen interest in how care could be extended so that, where it was appropriate, people could remain in their own homes during the last few days of their life. Moving to West Cumbria, she found what she describes as 'an infinitely mobile hospice which can be taken almost anywhere'. As she sometimes tells NHS audiences: 'People often say, "Where are your beds?" I say that we potentially have 140,000 beds!'

As she points out, in-patient hospices can provide a wonderful environment for people who are terminally ill. Inevitably, however, only a small minority of people are able to benefit from this service; nationally, about 17% of all patients with cancer die in hospices. The majority of cancer patients (about 55%) die in hospitals, typically on general acute hospital wards. However much effort and care the nursing staff on these wards put in, the pressures of hospital life and the relative anonymity of a large public ward makes this a far from ideal place for a dying person to be brought.

Given the choice, most patients say that they would prefer to face death in their own homes. Currently, however, less than one in three people with terminal cancer manages to achieve this. The point is usually not that they need treatment which only hospital can offer, but rather that they or the family member who is caring for them feel that care at home is no longer sustainable. With an adequate service for delivering palliative care nursing and for offering family carers a break, this situation could be changed.

Eileen Palmer reinforces her argument by reference to a recent study[4] undertaken in Doncaster. This research suggests that in-patient hospices may be finding it difficult to reach out to all sections of the community. In particular, the study found that people in semi-skilled and unskilled occupations are much less likely to die in a hospice than those in higher social classes.

The figures, taken from a total of 831 cancer deaths studied, are striking: 15% of these were from social classes I and II, 24% from social class III and 61% from social classes IV and V. But these proportions were not reflected in the breakdown of those who ended their lives in hospices: 82% of these were from the first three social classes, and only 18% from classes IV and V. Instead, the latter group contributed 77% of the deaths which had taken place in hospital. To put it another way, the study suggested that the poorest people in our society are more likely to end up dying in a general hospital ward than in a hospice.

---

4. Anita Sims *et al.*, 'Social class variation in place of cancer death', *Palliative Medicine*, 11 (1997).

LIAISON WITH MEDICAL PROFESSIONALS

West Cumbria Hospice at Home is an attempt to enable more people to stay on in their own homes. But as Eileen Palmer readily accepts, the absence of a building makes her job harder in some respects.

'It was certainly much easier working in a building, and not just in terms of the facilities. For example, it's easier to pull a team together when they are under one roof,' she says. 'This style of working is very much more challenging. It involves a lot of lateral thinking.'

It also means that her role as Medical Director is different. In a traditional hospice, residents admitted as in-patients would be under the medical director's direct charge. With the Hospice at Home, patients remain in the clinical charge of their GP, with Eileen Palmer's role as consultant limited to being an advisory one. Though it would be surprising if her advice were to be disregarded by a GP, in theory it could be (and on very rare occasions it is).

Speaking tongue-in-cheek and as a retired GP to a medical audience in 1997, Brian Herd put the relationship like this: 'GPs are prickly characters, they talk about "my patient" and "clinical control". They dislike taking advice ... It's easier to take advice from another doctor, as long as it is not a partner, particularly if it was requested and no one is threatening to take over "their patient". Eileen is so skilful that they never feel a thing.'

Eileen Palmer's own version of this relationship is, as you would imagine, a diplomatic one. She stresses the value of working in partnership with local medical professionals to raise the levels of understanding and awareness of palliative medicine. As she puts it, the process should be an empowering one for GPs so that they are able to help more easily in the future when patients develop terminal illnesses.

From her first appointment, Eileen Palmer has made a point of communicating with the 80 or so local GPs in the area and of providing general palliative care education for junior hospital doctors, hospital nurses and trainee doctors.

PALLIATIVE CARE

So what precisely is meant by 'palliative care'? This is a relatively young medical specialism, which in large measure has emerged from the good practice pioneered in early hospices such as St Christopher's. The discipline now has its own specialist journal and professional association.

Unlike most branches of medicine, palliative care is not about attempting to cure disorders; it takes over when cures are not possible, but where the patient can still benefit enormously from medical care. As Eileen Palmer explains, the word 'palliative' itself comes from the Latin word for a cloak: 'So palliative medicine is aimed at cloaking, hiding symptoms,' she says.

To a great extent this involves pain control measures. Early palliative medicine practitioners working in some of the first hospices often savagely criticised the medical orthodoxy of the time which prescribed modest doses of painkillers only when patients were already experiencing pain. Dr Richard Lamerton, for example, writing in 1973, complained:

Doctors who otherwise pride themselves on careful diagnosis followed by rational and precise treatment so often seem to sink into a mire of mythology and emotions when faced with a dying patient ... Patients are ignored when they most need attention, deceived when they most need someone with the courage to face their predicament with them and, worst of all, left in pain because the doctor fears to use the analgesics readily available to him.[5]

In particular doctors frequently underprescribed morphine-based painkillers in the fear that too high a dosage could be addictive. As hospice-based doctors pointed out, in the circumstances of a person with little time left to live but suffering from acute pain, this was a rather unnecessary concern.

Palliative medicine attempts to ensure that patients do not suffer the terrible pain which can accompany a serious illness by ensuring that painkillers are prescribed regularly and before the pain itself is felt. The techniques are still not as widely known as they should be, however. A paper published in 1995 which studied over 2,000 cancer deaths found that 88% of people were reported to have been in pain, and 66% were said to have had 'very distressing' pain. Only about one in three hospital patients had had adequate treatment.[6]

Palliative care medicine is not simply concerned with pain control, however. Other symptoms which may accompany a terminal illness (sometimes as side-effects of painkilling drugs) include sickness and vomiting, breathlessness, depression and fear, and severe constipation.

---

5. Richard Lamerton, *Care of the Dying* (Priory Press, 1973, revised edn Penguin Books, 1980).

6. Julia Addington-Hall and Mark McCarthy, 'Dying from cancer: results of a national population-based investigation', *Palliative Medicine*, 9 (1995).

PALLIATIVE CARE AT HOSPICE AT HOME

Eileen Palmer works on a part-time basis as West Cumbria Hospice at Home's Medical Director, officially working five sessions for the Hospice (a session is three and a half hours; a consultant's notional full week is made up of 11 sessions). In addition, she undertakes a further three sessions as the palliative care consultant at the main district hospital, the West Cumberland Hospital at Whitehaven.

The hospital had planned to run its own palliative care unit, and a purpose-built building was constructed at the back of the hospital site. Unfortunately it was no sooner built than the Health Authority encountered a problem in finding revenue funding for the unit; instead, the building was found a new use, as a centre for young people with disabilities.

The hospital, does, however have a small palliative care section of four beds at the end of an ordinary hospital ward. Eileen Palmer oversees the palliative care of the patients in these beds, and also that of patients who can benefit from palliative care elsewhere in the hospital, and indeed those in local nursing homes or cottage hospitals. She also has the support of a part-time assistant palliative care doctor, currently Dr Tim Sowton.

While there is considerable overlap between those Hospice at Home patients who are referred to Eileen Palmer and those who are receiving home nursing care, there is no direct correlation. Some people may encounter the Hospice service only through a visit from Eileen Palmer, some may receive only the nursing service. Furthermore, some patients who later return to their homes may first meet Dr Palmer while they are in hospital. It means that making sense of the annual statistics becomes a difficult task. Nevertheless, in a typical year Eileen Palmer is likely to have about 150 patients. She makes on average about five home visits a week.

For a recent Hospice at Home AGM she provided a breakdown of the symptoms suffered by 157 patients. The major reasons for referral for palliative care were:

Pain control	71 (45%)
Nausea and vomiting	26 (17%)
Counselling/psychological	24 (15%)
Breathlessness/cough	21 (13%)
Swollen limbs/lymphoedema	14 (9%)
Constipation	10 (6%)
Confusion	10 (6%)

Most patients in need of palliative care suffer from at least two major symptoms.

West Cumbria Hospice at Home has taken particular steps to help patients suffering from lymphoedema, as we shall see in chapter 7.

FINDING THE FINANCE FOR THE MEDICAL DIRECTOR

West Cumbria Hospice at Home has now developed a very close working relationship with the local Health Authority and NHS Health Trust. Brian Herd describes it as a 'happy and creative partnership', adding, 'If there are creative tensions from time to time, so much the better.'

Under the current complicated financial arrangements the Hospice finds the finance not only for Eileen Palmer's work as its Medical Director but also for her three weekly sessions at West Cumberland Hospital; currently the cost of the assistant palliative care doctor also comes from the Hospice budget.

Fortunately, these costs (and additional costs of services such as the drop-in centres and day-care centres) can be met thanks to a NHS contribution to the charity, which in 1997-8 was £107,000. NHS funding makes up about a third of West Cumbria Hospice at Home's annual income, at present about £300,000 a year. In other words, the NHS is both supporting the Hospice's work, and in turn itself being supported.

5. THE NURSING SERVICE

MANAGING THE NURSING SERVICE

In recent months, an innovation has been introduced. Each Monday morning, Hospice at Home has what Eileen Palmer describes as the 'ward round'. Given that the Hospice patients are spread around many hundreds of square miles of West Cumbria, this clearly is not a typical hospital ward round. The intention behind it is similar, however: a chance to make time to review the medical progress of each person currently receiving care.

The ward round takes place in the tiny office in the Workington health centre where the Hospice at Home has its nursing base, with the patients represented by their names on a large whiteboard on one of the walls. The participants normally include not only Eileen Palmer but also the Macmillan nurses for the West Cumbria area, including the Hospice's current Nurse Manager Janet Ferguson.

In a traditional hospice, the overall management of the nursing service would be in the hands of the hospice matron or nurse manager. West Cumbria Hospice at Home has a similar post, which for the first ten years of its work was filled by Margaret Dowling. Margaret retired from the position (though not from her involvement as Vice-Chairman and Trustee of the Hospice) in the spring of 1998. Janet Ferguson joined Hospice at Home in the autumn of 1997, allowing a six-month transitional period. She moved down to West Cumbria from Aberdeen where she had also been involved in the issues raised by the care of people who are terminally ill, through her work for a project concerned with AIDS patients.

As in the case of Eileen Palmer, her working arrangement with Hospice at Home is a complex one. Three-fifths of her work is funded through the NHS, and involves the coordination of the Macmillan nursing service in West Cumbria (exactly the role that Margaret Dowling also undertook). The Hospice directly funds the remaining two-fifths of her post. This is a new development; during Margaret

Dr Eileen Palmer (centre) takes part in the Monday morning 'Hospice ward round' in the Workington health centre office.

Dowling's time as Nurse Manager, the Hospice did not directly pay for her work in coordinating the hospice nursing team, but was able to benefit from this being undertaken as part of her NHS Macmillan nursing work. In honour of its new financial commitment, Hospice at Home has given Janet Ferguson an additional title, of Hospice Matron.

Macmillan nurses, it will be recalled, are specialists able to offer advice and support for cancer patients and their families. In addition to Janet herself, West Cumbria currently has three other Macmillan nurses, two full-time and one part-time (the latter made possible by Hospice's part-funding of Janet's post). The Macmillan nurses, who divide the West Cumbria area between them on a geographical basis, have a role in identifying need for Hospice at Home nursing care for their patients. Each has access to the nurse bank information, and can call in Hospice nurses as and when they are needed.

Janet Ferguson has overall responsibility for coordinating the management of the nursing side of Hospice at Home. Among other things, this means ensuring that all the Hospice nurses and health care assistants are adequately trained and supported.

THE NURSE BANK

As we have seen, West Cumbria Hospice at Home makes use of a bank system of nurses. About 70 nurses have been recruited to the bank (although one of the Macmillan nurses is male, up to now all the Hospice nurses have been women; the Hospice would be happy to recruit male as well as female nurses, but none has yet come forward). The bank includes some people who work a full week of shifts for the Hospice, as well as others who work on a part-time basis. There is, of course, no guarantee that shifts will be available, and conversely no obligation on nurses to take shifts which they are offered; Janet Ferguson has on occasions had to ring through most of her list when emergency care is needed at short notice at popular times such as Friday nights.

The Hospice bank includes state registered nurses, state enrolled nurses and health care assistants. New members of the bank are recruited through local newspaper advertisements, with recruitment drives taking place every year or so as bank numbers gradually fall.

Janet tries to ensure that all her bank nurses are actively available to take work, not least because of the task of ensuring that each keeps their professional knowledge up-to-date. Typically, a new recruitment drive brings in applications from 25 nurses and health care assistants. After interviews perhaps 12 to 15 are eventually selected. Gillian Bickersteth,

Nurses support meeting chaired by Nurse Manager Janet Ferguson.

a relatively recent recruit to the Hospice at Home nurse bank, recalls some of the questions at her own interview: 'It included issues which you wouldn't necessarily think about ... How do you react to people who start smoking? How do you react to hostility, directed at you but not because of anything you've done? How do you cope with relatives who want to sit up all night? All these sorts of things.'

For the nurses involved, Hospice at Home nursing is an isolated way of working, which makes the arrangements for support and feedback particularly important. Janet Ferguson uses the phone a great deal for keeping in contact with her nurses, and for finding out from them how patients are faring. Because Hospice nurses are potentially working day and night seven days a week, there is a management challenge here in ensuring that support is available when it is needed – after, say, a nurse has faced a particularly difficult session. Nurses have Janet Ferguson's home phone number for these occasions, though being on call in this way can put a considerable burden on Janet herself. Nor does it deal with the issue of what to do when she is on holiday or otherwise unavailable. It is fair to say that Hospice at Home is still working out the most appropriate support structures for its nurses. One advantage is that Janet's three Macmillan nursing colleagues are also potentially able to help out in emergencies.

Apart from the informal one-to-one telephone support offered by Janet and her colleagues, every six weeks there are more formal support meetings for the team of nurses. These clearly play an important role in allowing the nurses to share their experiences and concerns with colleagues.

Hospice nurses receive five days of training (spread over a number of weeks) when they first join the bank. This includes drug administration, pain management, communication skills with patients, and procedures after a death. It also involves a refresher course in the correct moving and handling of patients; back problems are all too common among health service staff, and moving and handling is a major element of many nurses' training programmes.

Thereafter, three training days are organised by Janet Ferguson each year at West Cumberland Hospital. These are not compulsory but there is a strong presumption that nurses will make an effort to attend (they are paid for their time on these courses). The Hospice also periodically offers opportunities for further specialist study or training with external agencies; in these cases, nurses undertake the study in their own time but have their fees paid for them.

LOOKING AFTER THE NURSES

The NHS is rightly concerned with the physical and mental well-being of its own healthcare professionals in a service which is characterised by a great deal of pressure and stress. People who are involved in palliative medicine and care, and who are therefore spending much of their working time with people who are incurably ill and dying, might seem to have the additional burden of having to face a great deal of suffering and tragedy.

'It is very intense work to sit with someone who is dying, for eight hours, perhaps three days a week,' Janet Ferguson says. 'I think it has to be work which you choose to do. Some people can't do it for more than a period of time.'

A recent study suggested, however, that the stress of caring for terminally ill patients was often counterbalanced by the rewards and satisfaction of the work.[7] It reported:

Perhaps counter-intuitively, death and dying do not emerge as a major source of job stress among either doctors working full time in palliative care or among non-specialists, including general practitioners and junior hospital doctors. Death and dying is reported as particularly stressful by palliative care nurse specialists when the patient is young, when the nurse has formed a close relationship with the patient, or when several deaths occur in a short space of time.

---

7. Amanda Ramirez *et al.*, 'ABC of Palliative Care: The Carers', *British Medical Journal*, vol. 316 (17 January 1998).

Talking to West Cumbria Hospice at Home nurses confirms that the task of caring for children and younger patients can be particularly difficult. Some nurses in fact request that they are not asked to undertake shifts where the patient is a child – fortunately such cases are relatively unusual. In general, and to the extent that it is possible, Janet Ferguson tries to arrange for nurses to be sent to care for patients with whom they have some shared interests or background. Janet adds that she has a responsibility to try to ensure that nurses are not currently facing distressing events in their personal lives. 'We have to know what is happening in the nurses' own lives at home,' she says.

West Cumbria Hospice at Home arranges for nurses to make one bereavement visit to a family after death has occurred. Many nurses say that, in addition, they sometimes choose to attend the funerals of their patients, especially those for whom they have cared for some period of time. They say that they feel their presence is often particularly appreciated by family members. This is, however, a decision for nurses themselves and not an occasion when they would be present in a professional capacity.

RELATIONSHIP WITH THE OTHER NURSING SERVICES

Mention has already been made of the Macmillan nursing service and of Marie Curie nurses and it will also by now be clear that West Cumbria Hospice at Home works extremely closely with the NHS. But the exact role which each plays can be confusing, not least to patients and their families. It is worth trying to untangle the web.

Patients at home are under the direct care and responsibility of the primary health care team. This includes the GP, who has continuing responsibility for the medical care of his or her patient, and also the district nurse. The district nurse is a key figure, with a responsibility among other things to make out a care plan for each patient, in conjunction with the patients themselves and their families. Even if West Cumbria Hospice at Home has been asked to provide nursing cover, district nurses will continue to visit patients and to take primary responsibility for their nursing care. 'The district nurse still goes in, does the dressings or observations or whatever there is to be done, but she's got a case-load and may have 15 or 20 patients to see. The Hospice at Home nurse is there just dealing with that one household,' Margaret Dowling explains.

It may well be that the district nurse will visit during the daytime while the Hospice at Home nurse undertakes night shifts. On the other hand, if the district nurse's visit coincides with a Hospice at Home nursing shift, it can mean that there are two pairs of hands rather than one to move or turn a heavy patient. Patient notes are kept in their home, and are added to as appropriate by each nurse who visits or undertakes a nursing shift.

The launch of West Cumbria Hospice at Home could have created considerable tensions between the NHS primary health care team and the charity's own staff. Margaret Dowling made considerable efforts, particularly in the early days, to ensure that district nurses were properly consulted and informed of the Hospice's work. The message put across was that the Hospice was not attempting to supplant the district nurse's responsibility for, or overall control of, the nursing care of the patient: 'We've always stressed that we are an additional service, we're not taking over or pushing anyone out. That's the only way in which you could make this work,' Margaret Dowling says. This approach also means that the Hospice cannot be criticised for providing from voluntary income the sort of core service which is properly the responsibility of a state-funded health service.

Patients with cancer are also likely to receive a visit from one of West Cumbria's Macmillan nurses. There are, as we have seen, four Macmillan nurses, three full-time and one part-time, in the area, including Janet Ferguson herself.

Finally, mention must again be made of the Marie Curie nursing service. For most of the Hospice at Home's first ten years, Marie Curie nurses provided a welcome additional resource, undertaking the same direct nursing work as Hospice at Home nurses (though with the limitation that only cancer patients were eligible for the service). Marie Curie nurses were managed by Margaret Dowling as Macmillan Nurse Manager, who was responsible for their recruitment and training in conjunction with the Marie Curie service's own Regional Nurse Manager. In practice, many Hospice at Home nurses were also registered as Marie Curie nurses.

More recently, Marie Curie has restructured its service provision in the region, and within the West Cumbria area the charity has decided that, at least for the time being, its nurses will now undertake palliative nursing care only within hospitals.

6. THE VIEW FROM HOME

So far we have looked at the work of West Cumbria Hospice at Home from the point of view of those who provide the service. But what about the view from home? The Hospice exists to help people who find themselves coping with a serious illness, and their perspective is arguably the most important one of all.

The process of coming to terms with a disease such as cancer is one which many people might prefer not to discuss publicly and I therefore particularly appreciate the efforts made by a number of West Cumbria Hospice at Home patients and their relatives who were willing to share their thoughts during the preparation of this book. Names, when used, are with their permission.

AN ALTERNATIVE TO HOSPITAL

The service offered by West Cumbria Hospice at Home is something which Thora Dickie can compare directly with the more familiar hospice model, since her older sister spent the last three weeks of her life as an in-patient in a Lincolnshire hospice. 'Many times my sister asked to be taken home but with no one there to look after her this was not possible. I think in future the Hospice at Home idea will be favoured in place of hospice buildings and unfamiliar surroundings.'

Thora Dickie first came across Hospice at Home some years ago when she took part in a bridge session in support of the hospice's work, unaware that later she would find herself using the nursing service which she was supporting. She lives with her husband Bob in a pleasantly furnished bungalow in one of the smaller towns in West Cumbria, and says she always tries to approach life in a positive way. The last few months have been difficult, however. She has had breast cancer which has developed secondary complications and which has led

Opposite: A Hospice nurse (standing right) and two neighbours visit a recently bereaved carer (seated centre).

to a weakness in her bones, so that she now uses a wheelchair to get about. Fortunately, after an operation, she now has more strength in her legs and is better able to do things around the house.

However, early in 1998, as she was back at home after a period in hospital, her husband Bob was also diagnosed with cancer and needed to undergo treatment in the hospital in Carlisle. With her carer now himself needing care, the only alternative seemed to be for Thora Dickie herself to return to a hospital bed. 'That idea didn't please me at all. The prospect was pretty grim, but I had no idea that there was any alternative,' she says. It was her GP who suggested that Hospice at Home might be able to help her, and arranged for a referral.

Her husband was in hospital for ten days initially, and then for another period of some weeks. During this time Hospice at Home took over much of the direct nursing care which Thora Dickie still needed. For a time, she was effectively locked within her own home, dependent on the arrival of the nurses. 'They never left me on my own during that time,' she says. Hospice at Home complemented the district nursing service, so that district nurses would get her up and dressed in the mornings with Hospice nurses taking over from midday until the following morning. 'According to the district nurses, I was very unwell and I couldn't have stayed at home on my own,' she adds.

Thora Dickie has improved considerably since that time, but unfortunately hospice care was also needed by her husband after he came out of hospital. Bob's illness affected his ability to eat, necessitating feeding by nurses, a process which sometimes took several uncomfortable hours. Thora is full of admiration for the patience which the nurses brought to their work.

'There were days when I could not be positive, when the future seemed so daunting. When Bob came home, I had to call – often at short notice – to ask for more help,' she says. Fortunately since those low times, her husband has been helped by a course of radiotherapy, and both partners are now feeling a little better able to cope. The regular nursing care from Hospice at Home has now been discontinued. 'Without Hospice at Home, I do not know how we would have come through,' Thora says. 'It was marvellous to know there was always help and support to hand when needed.'

A few miles away from the Dickies' house, Hospice at Home has also been able to offer support to Geoffrey and Mary Stocks. Geoffrey Stocks received help from Margaret Dowling and the Macmillan nursing service 15 years ago when his first wife was ill with cancer, but now finds that he is the one in need of some support. He has a chronic heart complaint which causes breathing difficulties, and has had a number of operations. He is being looked after at home by his second wife, who is herself a nurse.

Mary Stocks says that, because of her nursing background, she initially felt loath to accept Hospice help. 'I took my time to come to terms with having someone else here. It was very strange at first, but I welcome the Hospice nursing service with open arms now,' she says. In fact, Mary's nursing knowledge meant that her nights were more disturbed than they would otherwise have been, since she was much more aware of her husband's breathing irregularities and what they could signify. Hospice at Home now provides some night cover for the Stocks, allowing Mary, on those days at least, to get a good night's sleep.

Hospice at Home has also been able to provide day nursing on particular occasions, for example to enable Mary Stocks to get away to attend regional meetings of a charity in which she is actively involved. 'It's about the quality of life – providing as much normality as possible,' she says.

These are almost exactly the same words as those used by David Gratton when, in the course of battling with the rare asbestos-related cancer mesothelioma, he spoke of his determination to try to be treated, and to act, as much as possible like a normal person.

A chartered engineer and successful businessman, David used some of the skills he had learned in business in his approach to the management of his own illness. He and his wife Barbara allowed the BBC to film them during his last illness for a moving short TV programme *Before I Die*, which was broadcast shortly after his death. The programme brings out David's determined efforts not to accept passively the onset of his cancer. Barbara Gratton says that initially he was reluctant to accept Hospice help, seeing it as an admission of defeat. But when nursing care became essential, Hospice at Home was able to provide night-time support and, in the last few days, 24-hour nursing care.

David Gratton had breathing difficulties which required daily deliveries of oxygen cylinders to the Grattons' house outside Cockermouth. He was also supplied with the necessary equipment to enable him to administer his own morphine-based painkillers. 'There was nothing which could have been done in the hospital which we couldn't do at home,' says Barbara.

She adds, 'I was absolutely determined that David would stay at home.' And indeed, after a five-year struggle against the mesothelioma, David was able to avoid having to spend the last few days in a hospital ward. He died at home in November 1996.

7. HOSPICE AT HOME'S OTHER SERVICES

DEVELOPING A DAY-CARE SERVICE

To a large extent the name West Cumbria Hospice at Home adequately explains the work the organisation undertakes. But in one respect it is misleading. Every Wednesday and Friday, in Whitehaven and Cockermouth respectively, Hospice at Home does have a space of its own. These are the days when the organisation runs its day-care service for patients.

The day-care centres were a very early initiative of the Hospice and have been run continuously since 1991. NHS funding, made available to the organisation, was the welcome initial incentive to develop this service. But Brian Herd sees the day-care centres as a valuable element of what a hospice – even a hospice without walls – should be offering. 'All the time we are working to be as good as conventional hospices. We don't want our patients to feel that they are being short-changed,' he says.

Traditional hospices often run day-care services where patients can go both for treatment and for social events. West Cumbria Hospice at Home has a similar approach, though with the emphasis on the social side. At Whitehaven the Hospice hires the lounge of a sheltered housing complex, which, though close to the district hospital, is perhaps not an ideal venue (the room feels a little like a nursing home). In Cockermouth, the hospice has the use of a purpose-built day-care centre. For some years, a Thursday day-care service was also run in Millom, down in the south of the West Cumbria area. However, this was withdrawn in 1994, due to a lack of numbers.

The Whitehaven and Cockermouth day-care centres follow a similar pattern, though there are subtle differences between the two – and not

Opposite: The Hospice's Cockermouth drop-in centre for the bereaved.

simply that bingo is a Whitehaven favourite while Cockermouth is more interested in dominoes. Perhaps because of the surroundings, the Whitehaven centre tends to attract predominantly older people. Cockermouth currently has a wider age range, including a group of younger patients (known to all as the Youth Club). Each day-care centre can take up to ten patients.

Christine Hodgson has been the day-care sister since the start of the service. As she points out, the day-care centres can help both the patients and their families: 'It's a day off for the carer as well. They can get on with all the things which need to be done at home,' she says.

The day-care service operates from 10.00 till 4.00, though the first volunteers are likely to turn up around 9.30. The Hospice at Home welcomes volunteer help during the day, and also relies on volunteer drivers to bring in those patients who cannot drive themselves, and to take them home again at the end of the afternoon. The patients themselves begin to arrive around 10.00.

Christine undertakes an informal nursing round during the morning, taking time to talk to each patient separately. Hospice at Home has recently reviewed the staffing arrangements for day care, and a staff nurse, Margaret Williams, is now also normally on duty. While some patients make their own way to the day-care sessions, the service is also used by people who have become wheelchair-bound or are otherwise in poor health.

Mornings tend to be a time for socialising. There are resources for craftwork available, and craft items made during the day-care sessions are a bonus element in the Hospice's fundraising. Lunch, around midday, is a communal experience: 'Christine, Margaret and the volunteers make the meal time a highlight of the day, with well-laid tables and a good meal and pleasant conversation – and often with a bottle of wine for good measure,' says Margaret Dowling.

After lunch comes a quiet time, followed by gentle exercises and a formal relaxation session, before the afternoon activities begin. These may include guest speakers or artistes: the day-care programme over the years has included performances by dance troupes, flower arranging demonstrations, slide shows by photographers, talks, and much more. The Hospice also benefits from visits from the Council for Music in Hospitals, a professional touring ensemble who give one or two concerts a year. When the weather is good, outings are also arranged to local places of interest such as St Bees Head and Whitehaven Harbour. The afternoon finishes with tea and cakes at around 3.00, before the volunteer drivers take the patients back to their own homes.

A vivid picture of events in a day-care centre (in this instance, the sessions at Millom, which no longer run) was painted by a volunteer, Toni Richards, in an issue of the Hospice at Home's newsletter:

Who can forget the local farmer who came in his wheelchair, in a lot of pain, leaving his sheep farm in the hands of his son, clasping his thick book of poems, so well thumbed and knowing most of them by heart. He would recite them with such pleasure and then finish by telling us one of his risqué jokes with much giggling! The retired schoolmaster who sat and gave us 'lessons' all day – unable to be anything else but what he always had been – up in front of a class and teaching. We had two elderly ladies with the same name coming at the same time – one who although nearly blind would have a baking day and bring us scones for our tea and tell us hair-raising tales of pre-war childbirth at which she assisted, the other whose deafness made conversation difficult but didn't stop her talking – whether at cross purposes or not! How they all became dear friends as well as patients.

New patients are normally referred to the day-care service by their GP, district nurse or Macmillan nurse, and Christine Hodgson always makes contact first with a home visit: '... so that patients have a familiar face the first time they come, and an understanding of how the day is organised,' she explains. As she points out, people can be naturally apprehensive about joining a group of strangers.

The figures show, however, that – once the initial ice has been broken – people continue to come to the day-care sessions. In the 12 months to March 1998, for example, Hospice at Home ran 103 sessions, with a total attendance of 617. Twenty-nine people took advantage of the service.

COMPLEMENTARY THERAPIES

The day-care sessions also provide an opportunity for the Hospice at Home to offer some elements of complementary therapeutic care for its patients (the preferred adjective is 'complementary' rather than 'alternative', reflecting the Hospice's belief that patients should not dismiss the benefits of conventional medicine). A massage therapist attends each day-care session and massage and aromatherapy have been found to be both enjoyable and beneficial to the people attending.

Occupational therapy is provided, for example through the opportunities to undertake craft work at the centres. However, other initiatives by Hospice at Home have been rather less successful: for a time, the day-care sessions offered the services of an art therapist, but this has now been discontinued. While some people who are fighting a serious illness find that art is a powerful medium to express their feelings, Hospice at Home's use of an art therapist seems not to have been particularly popular. Nevertheless, painting is still offered and occasionally taken up.

West Cumbria Hospice at Home has not yet developed further in the direction of complementary therapy, though Brian Herd says that the organisation hopes ultimately to provide a service for patients being cared for in their homes. Interestingly, however, within the Hospice's geographical area is the Centre for Complementary Care at Knott End in Eskdale, a private charity which runs a centre for healing in a beautiful part of the Lake District. The Centre coordinates a self-help monthly cancer support group, and some Hospice patients have chosen to make the journey there to take part. Two members from the Centre recently led a session at a training day organised by Janet Ferguson for her bank of Hospice nurses.

LYMPHOEDEMA SERVICE

Christine Hodgson and Margaret Williams have an additional role in West Cumbria Hospice at Home, and that is to run the lymphoedema clinic operated by the Hospice. Previously, patients had to go to Newcastle-upon-Tyne, 90 miles away, for their treatment.

Lymphoedema can have a number of causes, but is often a secondary complication in cases of cancer and cancer treatment. Blockages in the lymphatic system, the network of vessels which conveys the lymph fluid to the venous system, cause the fluid to collect in one place leading to swelling, typically in the arms and legs. The swelling can be unpleasant and sometimes painful, and may also lead to a loss of ability to use to the full the arm or leg affected.

Fortunately the discomfort can often be relieved and the swelling controlled. Christine and Margaret have undertaken training in treatment techniques for lymphoedema, which include gentle massage, the use of special compression leg- and arm-stockings, and bandaging. Between them they staff the twice-monthly clinic, held at the West Cumberland Hospital outpatients' department. One of these is for new patients, who are seen for assessment both by Eileen Palmer and the nurses. The second clinic, for existing patients, is nurse-led.

Over 60 people were seen at the clinic during the 1997-8 Hospice year. In addition, a small number of patients were seen in their own homes for lymphoedema treatment. A further small number of in-patients in hospitals were provided with this service by the Hospice.

Nurse Christine Hodgson with a patient at the lymphoedema clinic operated by the Hospice at West Cumberland Hospital.

THE DROP-IN SESSIONS

Another initiative launched by Hospice at Home at the same time as the day-care service was the idea of 'drop-in' sessions for advice, information and bereavement support. Currently these are held once a week in both Cockermouth and Whitehaven. Each session runs for two hours, and is staffed by two Hospice nurses and by one of the Macmillan nurses.

The drop-in sessions are normally attended by about 20 to 30 people. Although they are available to patients, in practice it is mainly the bereaved who come for support and a cup of tea or coffee.

After several years, the sessions seem from the outside almost to have developed into social clubs, with their own groups of regulars. But Margaret Dowling says that this impression is misleading: 'A lot of self-help between the bereaved goes on, with those who have been bereaved for some time helping the newly bereaved when they come. All know that the nurses are there for them if they need a private word at a particularly difficult time,' she says.

EQUIPMENT SUPPLY

Hospice at Home has gradually built up a bank of medical equipment and nursing aids which it can make available to its patients. The list is a long one; it includes a range of different kinds of mattresses (to prevent pressure sores and provide comfort), cushions and pillows, bed cradles (to relieve the pressure of bedclothes on feet), bed tables and commodes. TENS (transcutaneous electrical nerve stimulation) machines are useful in pain relief. The Hospice can also provide nebulisers, which help people with breathing difficulties and can also be used for administering drugs, and syringe drivers (for administering pain-relieving drugs).

There are some less obvious items on the Hospice list. For example, baby alarms can be lent to patients and their families: this may seem of only limited value to a sick patient, but can make a tremendous difference to their carer if it saves a lot of to-ing and fro-ing up and down stairs.

Electric fans are also available: these obviously help to keep people cool during hot weather but have the added advantage of assisting breathing. And the Hospice has access to food mixers, which can be a

Opposite: Bereavement support at the Hospice's drop-in centre at Whitehaven.

Volunteer Coordinator Jane Bowden (foreground) organises the work of the Hospice's volunteers.

necessary kitchen item for patients who are no longer able to deal with ordinary meals.

West Cumbria Hospice at Home's bank of equipment, most of which is currently stored at the Workington health centre where the nursing office is also based, has been built up primarily thanks to gifts from individuals and organisations. It is, of course, a fact of fundraising life that it is easier to appeal to donors for particular items than for ongoing revenue needs.

8. THE VOLUNTEERS

It will already be clear that there are different facets to the work of West Cumbria Hospice at Home, and different ways in which people come into contact with the organisation. The role of volunteers at the day-care centres was mentioned in the last chapter; it is now time to explore this element further.

About 35 people work as volunteers for West Cumbria Hospice at Home, some on a regular weekly basis and others more infrequently. The Hospice at Home began to use volunteers at the same time as it launched the day-care centres initiative, and it is still at the two day-care sessions in Whitehaven and Cockermouth that the volunteers make their greatest contribution.

There is nothing *ad hoc* about the arrangements. Hospice at Home volunteers have been interviewed and trained, in much the same way as the nurses in the bank system used for nursing care. Volunteer rotas are drawn up on a bi-monthly basis, so that each person knows well in advance when they will be needed on duty.

The work of organising the volunteers is undertaken by Jane Bowden. Jane, who works out of the offices in the Workington health centre, initially joined Hospice at Home at the start of 1991 as the organisation's full-time secretary. By May 1991, NHS funding for the day-care sessions meant that Jane's role could be developed and since that time she has spent half her time undertaking the job of Volunteer Coordinator. A part-time colleague has joined her, to compensate for the time she can no longer spend on secretarial work.

Building up the team of volunteers is not quite as straightforward as might be imagined. 'It's not easy to get the right people, and it's always difficult to interview people and then say no,' Jane says. Generally speaking, the Hospice does not take volunteers who have been bereaved in the past 12 months. The feeling is that volunteering for the Hospice is not really advisable as a way of getting over a bereavement.

New volunteers tend to be recruited by word of mouth, though Hospice at Home has also put up notices in GP surgeries and made use of the local volunteer bureaux. The process of recruitment usually starts as a phone call, when Jane Bowden explains informally what the work involves. This is followed up with an application form and then by an interview ('a jolly affair, notwithstanding a certain shrewdness behind the smiles', according to one recruit) for which Jane Bowden is normally joined by Christine Hodgson, a Hospice day-care sister. References are also taken up.

Many volunteers are retired (Hospice at Home is fortunate that many are retired nurses), though there are also some younger volunteers. Some are young people planning to follow a nursing career.

Volunteers are given training both before starting work and regularly thereafter. There are relatively formal sessions, held at West Cumberland Hospital, which include issues of hygiene, confidentiality, and moving and handling techniques. There are also regular support meetings for the volunteer team, usually held from 10.00 to 3.00 about three times a year, which provide an opportunity for ongoing training in a more informal environment. Typically, issues covered at these gatherings will include interpersonal skills communication and techniques for coping with difficult situations. Training is coordinated by Jane Bowden.

In its use of volunteers, West Cumbria Hospice at Home has perhaps chosen a more conservative approach than some in-patient hospices, which can have very large teams of volunteers. Up to now it has not used volunteers for its home-based work. This is an option which has been discussed and rejected a number of times in the past, though the issue remains under review. Jane Bowden herself feels that home-based volunteer work could be successful, and certainly some other hospices have experience of using volunteers in the home setting. But there are clearly also difficulties: as Brian Herd points out, 'These days you've got to think about what would happen if something goes wrong.' Voluntary organisations generally have a wide range of issues to consider when they make use of volunteers, including legal, employment, health and safety, insurance and tax matters.

At present, therefore, West Cumbria Hospice at Home volunteers concentrate their efforts on the Whitehaven and Cockermouth day-care sessions. Toni Richards (whose account of the Millom centre was quoted in the last chapter) should perhaps have the last word: 'If you can play dominoes, cards, call for bingo, run quizzes, knit, wash up but above all LISTEN – you may be a good candidate for the team!'

9. FINDING THE FUNDS

HELPING THE HOSPICE BY REMEMBERING THE PAST

John Skelly lives with his wife in Whitehaven, up on the cliffs close to the sea in what was once a row of miners' terraced houses. John, who is in fine health at the age of 84, was himself a miner for the whole of his working life. John Skelly was brought up in Whitehaven and left school at 14 to work first at nearby Wellington Pit. ('I was a good scholar at school, but I was wanted for earning, not learning; it was difficult for most miners' children to go to grammar school.') He eventually became the Under-Manager of another Whitehaven pit, Haig Pit, having declined to take a management job until after nationalisation. He talks of the comradeship and strong community ties brought about by adversity, but is also critical of the poverty suffered by miners: 'Pain is a bad master, whether it is physical pain or the pain of poverty,' he says.

The coal seams of the West Cumberland coalfields are now worked no more, but in their time brought employment and (for the owners at least) prosperity to this geographically isolated part of northern England. John Skelly was following the path taken by his father, James, who also worked as a miner.

The physical reminders of the coal mining industry (and of the nearby iron and steel industry) are ever present in the urban and rural landscapes of West Cumbria. Here are the sites of the pits, here the housing erected to provide accommodation for the workers, here the ports where the coal was taken away. But the human memories of this important period of Cumbria's history are not so easy to find. As John himself knows, the men who experienced life as miners are now growing older and there are certainly very few like him whose memories stretch back to the 1920s.

John Skelly is concerned to record that history. His recent book, *Poems of the Pits*, is an anthology of about 40 poems exploring aspects of the miners' lives. The book itself is 'dedicated to the brave company of

Remembering the past: retired miner John Skelly, former Under-Manager of the Haig Pit at Whitehaven, donates the takings from the sale of his poetry to the Hospice at Home.

miners who faced much that was unknown and undesired in their search for a livelihood'. The book has been successful, already selling over 1,300 copies, and that success has had a very welcome side-effect: John is donating all the takings to West Cumbria Hospice at Home.

The poem *The Narrow Way*, taken from his anthology, is typical of the way he tries to record this element of the region's history:

> The miner is used to the narrow way,
> It begins when he leaves sight of the sky
> And drops down that brick-lined shaft
> And waves wide space goodbye ...
>
> Where he works is narrow,
> He's surrounded by coal and stone,
> His thoughts are narrowed, to major things,
> His work, the danger, his home.
>
> He's oft hemmed in by prejudice
> With those of narrow view
> Who think of a miner down below,
> And would keep him down there too.
>
> He's been hemmed in by economics,
> The pennies and the pounds.
> His narrow earnings left small chance
> To share in the social round.
>
> Yes narrow indeed has been the road
> And limited his choices,
> But none can equal his brave heart
> Mid all the world's loud voices.

Most of the cost of publishing *Poems of the Pits* was met by two charitable trusts, which has meant that he has been able to give £3,300 to the Hospice. West Cumbria Hospice at Home has also benefited from two earlier books which John Skelly has written, a memoir of his childhood *Through my Time Telescope* and reminiscences of his youth *Sights and Sounds of the 1920s*, which together have brought in almost £5,000 more.

Why is John Skelly supporting Hospice at Home? He has had no direct or indirect experience of the nursing work which the Hospice undertakes, and indeed has had only very limited contact with the organisation at all – normally he gets in touch only when he has a cheque to hand over. He says that it just seems to him the right thing to do.

THE FUNDRAISING ROUND

West Cumbria Hospice at Home benefits from donations from all sorts of people, and from all sorts of things that they do in the cause of fundraising. For example, a more contemporary side of Whitehaven life from that recorded in John Skelly's books is seen in the regular American line dancing sessions which are held in the town's Civic Hall; but the profits from these too are given to the Hospice. If line dancing is too energetic, what about dominoes? The Anchor Vaults pub in Whitehaven recently sent in a cheque for £210 collected at the regular domino evenings.

In the course of a typical year, about £70,000 will be raised from donations and from fundraising events. This averages out at about £1,400 for each week of the year, a considerable amount for an area which is not particularly affluent.

Little by little the money comes in. The Hospice annual reports and newsletters give some sense of the size and variety of all the fundraising work:

Annie Southam is still going strong bingo-wise ... since June she has contributed a further £1,070 ... Gosforth Friends held their usual Easter Coffee Day raising £374 ... St Bees group were able to send £900 to the Treasurer following a splendid Gilbert and Sullivan concert ... Table top sales are now a regular and profitable event on the calendar at Calderbridge ...

A busy day at Ravenglass Charter fair with a good result – £210 ... Seascale group visited Muncaster Country Fair with the tombola: £440 ... a guided walk across Morecambe Bay was enjoyed by several members – a good paddle was enjoyed by all: £283 ...

Elizabeth Smith and her Youth Choir entertained us at Gosforth ... West Cumbria Motor Cycle Club held a sponsored Ride Out on behalf of the charity: the club have contributed almost £2,000 to Hospice at Home and hope to repeat the event annually! ...

The weather did not favour the Seascale and Gosforth Garden Fete which had to be held indoors. The weather was not allowed to dampen the spirits, we had an excellent day and raised £1,007 ...

A regular annual Brass Band Concert in Christ Church, Maryport, was used as a venue for an Anniversary raffle by the Maryport Group ... An Embleton lady organised a professional flower demonstration at Moota Motel ... Pyramid coffee mornings are a new venture and proving very successful ...

Opposite: A fundraising coffee morning at Gosforth arranged by the South Forum group.

Flimby Male Voice Choice and guest soloists performed an excellent evening of Midsummer Music at Cockermouth Castle ...

This year the prize for the most unusual (event) must go to the Sponsored Juggle up Skiddaw ...

And so it goes on. Here, page after page, is not only a record of the hard work put in by so many people to bring in the pounds and pennies, but perhaps of something more profound: an insight into the health of community life in this part of England, a vast net of social activity providing the glue which holds people together in their towns and villages.

STRUCTURES FOR FUNDRAISING

The impression may be one of spontaneity and individual enterprise, but as you might imagine, West Cumbria Hospice at Home does not leave its fundraising to chance. For fundraising purposes, the Hospice has divided its area into two and has established a North Forum and a South Forum. These are informal groups which bring together active Hospice fundraisers, providing an opportunity for them to coordinate their programmes and support each other's ventures. The rationale behind this arrangement was set out in the Hospice's 1997 annual report:

It is our belief that local people know best what makes their community tick, what fundraising ideas will be successful and how to maximise their potential income. This is why, wherever possible, ideas and coordination for fundraising should come from the grassroots. However it is recognised that individual Friends Groups need to have a support network which gives the opportunity to exchange ideas and most importantly the opportunity to plan combined fundraising activities.

The North area has active groups in Cockermouth and Maryport, organising many local events, but it is in the South that the Forum idea has worked particularly successfully. Meetings typically take place every two months, and are regularly attended by more than 20 people.

Joe and Mary Smith are among those who actively participate in these meetings. The Smiths live in the small village of Gosforth, close to the BNFL plant at Sellafield, and their interest in West Cumbria Hospice at Home is immediately evident to visitors to their house: beside the garden gate is a noticeboard which lists all the forthcoming fundraising events in the area. Inside there is further evidence, not least the large piles of goods waiting for the next tombola or table-top sale to be held.

The Smiths are both retired, Joe from his job as a policeman. 'You've been working all your life and suddenly you find that you've got time on your hands, so you put it to good use,' he says. 'My poor garden is neglected, we've been so busy,' adds Mary. It might be thought that the task of fundraising for a hospice without walls would be more difficult than getting support for a similar venture based in a physical building. The Smiths, however, argue that this is not the case: 'No, it works in our favour: there's no white elephant to maintain,' Joe says. 'If you're terminally ill, the place you want to be is at home with the family. I think it prolongs life a little.' His wife adds, 'I think it's a brilliant idea for an area like this.'

The overall responsibility for watching over the fundraising efforts of the South Forum has been taken by one of the Hospice Trustees, Felicity Watson. (Felicity, it will be remembered was the Nurse Manager who first set up the Macmillan service in West Cumbria, and who spoke at the very first Hospice public meeting.) She is aware of the importance of integrating the work of the fundraising teams with the nursing and medical side of the Hospice. 'The fundraisers are excellent, and their ideas are excellent. They deserve to know how the money they raise is being spent. Equally, the people who are spending the money need to know the effort that goes into raising the money,' she says.

She knows that the Hospice's need for fundraising help is one which will never go away. 'We need to be careful not to rest on our laurels. Yes, we have now got the key underpinnings of a hospice service. But the day we think we're done is the day that we start to fail.'

10. Managing the Charity

MANAGING THE MONEY

At every annual general meeting of every voluntary organisation there is a moment in the proceedings, probably marked by a flurry of papers as those in the audience try to find the right documents, when the treasurer gets up to present the accounts.

A few will carefully scrutinise the dense columns of figures, nod knowingly as the treasurer explains the year's income and expenditure and perhaps interject with the odd perceptive question; the majority, on the other hand, will say nothing, probably silently thanking their stars that their organisation has got somebody else to concern themselves with the money.

It can be a thankless task being treasurer of a voluntary organisation. It can certainly be a big responsibility if your organisation has registered charity status, not least because in recent years the charity will have had to amplify and extend the accounts produced to meet the rigorous new accountancy Statement of Recommended Practice (SORP) guidelines. And if your charity has the sort of turnover which would satisfy many a small business, the work and responsibility are obviously compounded.

The person who stands up each year to present the accounts at West Cumbria Hospice at Home's AGMs is Michael Roberts. Fortunately for the Hospice, Michael is a retired chartered accountant. Fortunately, too, he has been actively involved as Honorary Treasurer since the very start of the Hospice venture. He wryly recounts the story of how Brian Herd, who was his GP at the time, recruited him to the cause back in February 1987. Michael himself had recently been in hospital for an operation when Brian Herd approached him to ask him to consider becoming the Hospice's Treasurer: 'He got me when I was at my weakest!' Michael says.

The accounts which Michael Roberts was able to present to the 1998 AGM show a charity in rude financial health. From a standing start and over a period of only 11 years, West Cumbria Hospice at Home has

Guiding spirits: Dr Brian Herd and Margaret Dowling (Chairman and Vice-Chairman of the Hospice at Home), with Hospice Nurse Manager Janet Ferguson (centre).

managed to husband its resources and build up its reserves so that its financial position is now guaranteed, at least for the foreseeable future. Even if all its fundraisers suddenly packed up and left the area, if not a penny more came in in donations and if the NHS abruptly decided to cut its funding, the Hospice would still be able to run its service unaffected for at least two more years. Such is the measure of the financial strength which West Cumbria Hospice at Home has now achieved.

West Cumbria Hospice at Home's annual income, from all sources, is currently about £330,000 – or almost exactly a third of a million pounds. One-third of this (just under £110,000) comes as a financial contribution from the NHS, now made not as a grant but under a contractual arrangement for the work which the Hospice undertakes. The remainder the Hospice has to raise by its own efforts.

The most important source of income is, of course, fundraising. As we saw in the last chapter, West Cumbria Hospice at Home supporters manage to raise approximately £70,000 each year from fundraising events and donations.

The accounts itemise separately the additional gifts which the Hospice at Home receives in legacies and bequests. This can be an important source of income for hospices, but, as treasurers know, it can also be a very unpredictable element in a charity's accounts. For two years in the mid-1990s, for example, the legacy income for West Cumbria Hospice at Home was more or less stable at about £60,000 a year. This, however, followed a year when only £12,000 had come in. In 1997-8 legacy income increased to over £80,000, but almost half of this came from a single very generous bequest. West Cumbria Hospice at Home also separately records donations which have been made *in memoriam* – perhaps where a family has asked for gifts to the Hospice instead of flowers at a funeral. These average a further £15,000-£20,000 in most years.

The only other substantial source of income for West Cumbria Hospice at Home is the interest which it obtains on its investments. Year by year, the Hospice has managed to put money aside to build up its reserves, which now stand at around £700,000. The investment income is a welcome fillip and for the 1997-8 year was almost £45,000.

How does the Hospice at Home spend its money? Charities these days have to separate in their accounts the expenditure they have made for charitable purposes and the money spent on administration. Only about £11,000 of West Cumbria Hospice at Home's £330,000 income goes on management and administration.

By far the biggest item of expenditure is the home nursing service. For the 1997-8 year almost £170,000 was spent in this area; the bulk was spent on paying the salaries of the nurses undertaking the work. The next two largest areas of expenditure were the Hospice's medical services (including the costs of employing both Eileen Palmer and the assistant palliative care doctor) and the day-care service. In total, the Hospice's direct expenditure for charitable purposes for 1997-8 was approximately £290,000.

Mention has already been made of the NHS funding for West Cumbria Hospice at Home, which started in 1991. Initially £23,500, this was provided to launch and operate the day-care service. Fortunately, the amount of state funding was subsequently increased: by 1993-4, the funding had been raised to about £100,000 to cover not only the day-care service but also the cost of employing the Hospice's new Medical Director, and to make a contribution towards the home nursing service costs. Since then, NHS support has gradually increased to about £107,000.

However, this may give a slightly misleading impression since Hospice at Home recycles some of its NHS grant back into the Health Service. We have looked earlier in this book at the complex funding arrangement, for example, for the post of Medical Director. The Hospice also currently pays for the part-time assistant palliative care doctor, Tim Sowton. These arrangements currently satisfy both the local Health Trust and the Hospice, though it is possible that the NHS might in future take over the direct funding of some of this work.

One of the Hospice at Home's proud boasts is that it has never yet had to turn down a request for help because of a shortage of money. The foundations of its current strong financial position were laid in the first few years of its life. Fundraising got off to a flying start, with over £60,000 raised in the first year and over £100,000 the following year. Though the first patients were taken on very quickly, nevertheless at this stage the nursing service was still only a fledgling one. For example, in its second year of operation, 1988-9, only about £28,000 was spent on the nursing service. This meant that the bulk of the money raised could be transferred straight into the Hospice's reserves.

In some respects, this is a pattern which most new in-patient hospices also follow in their first years of life, as they build up the reserves they need to build or convert the hospice building. Had it so wished, West Cumbria Hospice at Home would probably have been in a financial position by the early 1990s to proceed with a building project. If it had done so, however, its balance sheet today would show a rather different picture, without the large cash reserves now built up (and without the corresponding high investment income which it receives). 'I think we would have been struggling to provide a building and the actual nursing service as well,' Michael Roberts says.

DAY–TO–DAY FINANCIAL ADMINISTRATION

For the first ten years of its life, West Cumbria Hospice at Home's financial records took up a substantial part of a room in Michael Roberts's house. Recently, the Hospice has reconsidered this arrangement, and in the spring of 1997 rented a small office in a business centre in Cockermouth.

Michael Roberts retired from his accountancy business in 1992, but is as active as ever in sorting out the Hospice's financial affairs. He comes in most mornings to the Cockermouth office, though he does now have some part-time paid help from a former employee of his company who works for the Hospice 12 hours a week. The Hospice has recently computerised its accounting procedures.

In one respect, West Cumbria Hospice at Home benefits from its close relationship with the local Health Trust. The substantial payroll work associated with employing up to 70 nurses is handled for the Hospice by the Trust, without charge.

THE WORK OF THE SECRETARY

If much of the hard slog of administering the Hospice's finances goes on out of sight, the same is equally true of other administrative work. The Hospice's Honorary Secretary since its beginning has been Jack Frearson, and Hospice-related correspondence takes up a large amount both of his time and of space in his home.

Jack Frearson joined the Merchant Navy in 1939, and saw exciting times in the Atlantic and Mediterranean convoys during the war years. Subsequently he spent almost 20 years in Calcutta, as a partner in a firm of stevedores, before returning to Britain to end his career as Chief Marketing Manager for the Port of Liverpool. He and his wife retired to Cumbria, where he still enjoys recreational sailing. Jack Frearson's work provides the glue to hold the Hospice administration together. It is he, for example, who keeps in touch with the Hospice's supporters, and ensures that they are thanked for their fundraising efforts and donations. This may seem a detail, but nevertheless it is one which ensures that the Hospice's reputation in its own community continues to be high.

Other, more substantial, areas of work have had to be undertaken. West Cumbria Hospice at Home has applied on a number of occasions for funding from the National Lottery Charities Board for its work, though so far without success. 'One of the senior officers of the Charities Board admitted to me, "The allocation itself is something of a lottery!"' Jack Frearson says. Nevertheless, Hospice at Home is persevering, and anticipates making further applications for a share of National Lottery money.

THE TRUSTEES AND EXECUTIVE COMMITTEE

West Cumbria Hospice at Home is established by a trust deed and legally, therefore, its management is in the hands of the group of Trustees. Four of the Hospice's founding Trustees are still in post today: Brian Herd (Chairman), Margaret Dowling (Vice-Chairman), Jack Frearson and Felicity Watson. More recently they have been joined by two colleagues, Mary Todd (formerly the Hospice's legal adviser) and Peter Allen (before retirement, the NatWest bank manager in Cockermouth). When the Trustees meet they are joined by Graham Pratley (a local solicitor and the Hospice's new legal adviser) and by

Michael Roberts. This body is known as the Council.

West Cumbria Hospice at Home also has an Executive Committee, which provides an opportunity for supporters of the Hospice, especially those engaged in fundraising, to participate in the running of the charity. The Executive Committee currently has 13 members. It comprises the seven Council members and a further six additional members who are elected each year at the Hospice's AGM.

The Executive Committee, an advisory body, meets on a regular basis, usually about every six weeks. However, it is the Trustees who effectively act as an executive for the charity and who take the key strategic decisions, particularly those where there are financial, legal or employment implications. At present, members of the Council stay on after the end of every second Executive Committee meeting for their own brief meeting. Additional meetings of the Council are held on an *ad hoc* basis when they are necessary.

MEMBERSHIP OF THE HOSPICE

At this stage the question may be asked: who comes to AGMs and helps elect the Executive Committee members? The answer is that the Hospice has created a membership group for its friends and supporters, the West Cumbria Hospice at Home Association.

The decision to set up the Association was taken when the Hospice was first established. It is not primarily a fundraising initiative; membership, for many years fixed at £3, has recently been increased but only to a modest £5 a year. Members of the Association, as well as having the opportunity at AGMs to hear of the Hospice's developments, also receive the annual report and the newsletter. This combines news of the nursing and medical work of the Hospice with fundraising information. The Hospice currently has about 260 members, from across the whole West Cumbrian area.

11. TEN YEARS ON: THE HOSPICE AT HOME EXPERIENCE

SPREADING THE MESSAGE

By the time of its tenth birthday in 1997, West Cumbria Hospice at Home had developed into a mature organisation. 'We have moved from being a new organisation, providing hospice services in a novel way, to become a well-established hospice with a wealth of experience to pass on to others,' Brian Herd said at the AGM that year. Indeed, in recent years other hospice groups have increasingly begun to look to the West Cumbrian experience when planning their own services. The pioneering idea behind West Cumbria Hospice at Home's work, that of providing hospice care directly in patients' own homes, has been spreading.

Just to the east, for example, a home-based hospice service has developed in the North Lakeland area around Penrith. In Northumberland, the town of Hexham has been the focus for a similar project. Another hospice at home service has been developing over the Scottish border in Stranraer. Other visitors have come from further afield: from Wales and Ireland, for example, as well as – on two separate occasions – from Australia.

West Cumbria Hospice at Home decided to mark its anniversary by organising a national conference for medical professionals on the theme 'Hospice without Walls'. The conference was arranged for a date early in May 1997, and the venue was a hotel north of Keswick on the edge of the Lake District. The pre-publicity put it categorically:

Opposite: Hospice fundraisers – donations and fundraising events bring in about £70,000 of the Hospice at Home's annual revenue.

Most terminally ill patients wish to stay at home and most carers want to look after them at home. It is now possible to achieve this aim for the majority of patients by integrating the efforts of local and national charities with the NHS.

Conference delegates had a varied programme. Professor Eric Wilkes, a leading figure in the development of palliative care medicine, began by offering a historical perspective. His presence was perhaps particularly appropriate: long before West Cumbria Hospice at Home had been set up, he had visited the West Cumbria region and met Margaret Dowling and other Macmillan nurses. Margaret recalls how, even at that stage, he had suggested that if and when West Cumbria began to consider creating a hospice it should look seriously at the idea of a hospice at home.

Dr Anne Naysmith from Paddington Community Hospital gave a presentation on the work of caring for AIDS patients at home. There were contributions on home-based care of the terminally ill in Newcastle-upon-Tyne, and indeed around the world. But – as you would expect – the conference also provided an opportunity for Brian Herd, Eileen Palmer and Margaret Dowling jointly to tell delegates about their own experience.

THE COSTS AND BENEFITS

Brian Herd's presentation included a look at the costs and benefits of the Hospice at Home service for the NHS. As he pointed out, some benefits, such as improving the quality of life of the dying, and reducing the strain felt by carers, are unquantifiable.

But he also shared with the audience the results of a survey he had previously undertaken. This built on research he had carried out in 1987, just before the Hospice at Home nursing service had begun. His research surveyed in detail (over a 22-week period) the place of death for 157 patients in West Cumbria suffering from terminal cancer.[8] Five years later, in 1992, Brian Herd had conducted a similar survey, this time of 188 patients over a 26-week period.

By comparing the two, Brian Herd hoped to be able to see if the existence of Hospice at Home had had any marked effect on the use of hospital beds in the area. The study did indeed show a reduction in the number of deaths in hospital, though the fall was relatively small – from 47% in 1987 to 43% in 1992. Rather more significant, however, was the

---

8. EB Herd, 'Terminal care in a semi-rural area', *British Journal of General Practice*, 40 (1990), pp. 248-51.

comparison of time spent in hospital. In 1987, the average time spent in hospital by patients before their death had been 23.6 days. In 1992 this was down to 14.5 days. For the record, the full details are as follows:

	1987	1992
Number of patients	157	188
Hospital deaths	74 (47.1%)	81 (43.1%)
Final admissions (mean duration)	23.6 days	14.5 days

From this survey, Brian Herd extrapolated the change in the total annual number of bed days required per year in West Cumbria. This suggested that, in 1992, the NHS had effectively saved the equivalent of 1,790 bed days for patients in the terminal stages of cancer, compared with the situation in 1988.

The cost to the NHS of hospital beds is enormously high. In 1992, for example, the average daily hospital cost in West Cumbria per patient was between £116 and £202, with a weighted average of £140. A simple multiplication of £140 by 1,790 led Brian Herd to the finding that the notional saving to the NHS in 1992 was £250,600. As he pointed out, the total expenditure by West Cumbria Hospice at Home in 1992 was only about half this amount, or £132,000.

In other words, Brian Herd's argument is that West Cumbria Hospice at Home, whatever else it achieves, also makes financial sense. 'It appears, almost as a side-effect, that the charity is saving NHS resources,' he told his conference audience. 'Providing nurses on a one-to-one basis sounds extravagant. In fact, it is more cost-effective than staffing an in-patient unit. Our nurses are engaged for just the number of hours needed. A unit remains fully staffed even if half-empty.'

This is an interesting conclusion. If the findings are correct, a home nursing care service not only enables more people to be at home at the moment of death but also means that those who are admitted to hospital are there for a much shorter period of time, and that there is a reduced need for respite (non-medical) admissions.

COMPARISON WITH RESIDENTIAL HOSPICES

But how does the home hospice service provided in West Cumbria compare in cost/benefit terms with more conventional residential hospices?

This is a more difficult question to answer, not helped by the fact that each of the independent local hospices produces its own sets of accounts, using different ways to account for the costs of the various different services being provided. Somewhat surprisingly, there has been little attempt to bring together this information on a comparative basis nationally, though a pilot project, under the auspices of the National Council for Hospice and Specialist Palliative Care Services, which is examining the way that 11 local hospices record and analyse their costs, is currently under way.

Let us start with the results of a survey carried out by the National Council in 1997 which found that the expenditure budgets of 146 voluntary hospices broke down as follows:

Over £5m	2 hospices
£2m–£5m	25
£1m–£2m	38
£0.5m–£1m	44
below £0.5m	37

These expenditure figures include the cost not only of residential facilities but also of other hospice services.

As we have seen, West Cumbria Hospice at Home was able to launch its nursing service very quickly, without having to engage in the lengthy fundraising which most hospices have to undertake to meet initial capital costs. Brian Herd estimates that, at the time when West Cumbria Hospice at Home began, a new-build 12-bed hospice would probably have cost about £750,000. Today a figure between £1m and £2m seems realistic. By not needing to invest in bricks and mortar, West Cumbria Hospice at Home was able to build up substantial reserves very quickly. These in turn now produce substantial annual interest payments.

A residential hospice also has to meet the ongoing revenue costs associated with maintaining and staffing a building. One recent comparative study of a small number of Midlands hospices found that in 1996-7 the average cost per occupied bed per day varied from £167 to £248 (because of the high degree of nursing and medical care provided in a hospice, these costs are higher than those for in-patient NHS hospital beds).

Allowing for some degree of under-occupancy of beds, this suggests that a small hospice with a dozen beds would have to raise perhaps £550,000–£800,000 a year to meet its costs. With hospices typically receiving a third of their funding from the NHS, this leaves a very substantial amount of money to be found from voluntary sources.

Clearly, it is much more expensive for a hospice to care for people on an in-patient basis than in their own homes. But this perhaps misses the point. Hospices aim to do the best they can for those who are dying, and if this means the provision of care in an in-patient environment then it will be right to pursue every avenue to raise the money necessary. West Cumbria Hospice at Home argues, however, that many people who are approaching death are anxious to remain in the familiar surroundings of home. In-patient care may be required where there are medical needs which can be met only in a hospital or a residential hospice. But the presumption should be in favour of letting people stay at home. As West Cumbria Hospice at Home demonstrates, it is surprising just how much medical and nursing care can be delivered to the home, if the structures and will are there.

A MODEL FOR OTHERS?

Is West Cumbria Hospice at Home, therefore, a model for others to adopt? Certainly in a large geographical area with a dispersed population, such as the West Cumbrian coastal plain, it seems unlikely that a single hospice building could adequately meet the needs of the whole community.

Brian Herd believes that the model of a hospice at home service is valid not only in rural areas; he argues that the idea could be copied in urban areas as well. Indeed, many city-based hospices do offer a home-based service to patients, though this does not always extend to the sort of fully-fledged nursing service offered by West Cumbria Hospice at Home. Brian Herd does accept, however, that there may be different circumstances to take into account in other areas. As he points out, large cities do not always have the close family networks of a settled community such as West Cumbria – and a hospice at home service does depend on family members or friends being close at hand to act as informal carers for the person who is ill.

A hospice at home also needs nurses. Brian Herd says that West Cumbria Hospice at Home has benefited from being based in an area where a pool of experienced nurses is available to be recruited. He is aware that this is not always the case throughout the country.

Nevertheless, it seems clear that there are considerable opportunities to develop further the idea of home-based hospice care. The work in West Cumbria has proved this to be a much-needed service for patients and their families and one which it does not take enormous financial resources to achieve.

At the Hospice drop-in centre at Whitehaven.

12. CONCLUSION

The last chapter included some thoughts on the work of West Cumbria Hospice at Home contributed by Brian Herd. It seems appropriate to begin this one with a remark from Margaret Dowling, the other person who has done so much to steer the charity forward in the years since 1987:

Occasionally we still get a few people who say, 'We don't have a Hospice in West Cumbria, do we?' My answer is that we do have a Hospice, and a very successful Hospice; what we don't have is a building. Hospice is a philosophy of care, not a building.

It should by now be clear that West Cumbria Hospice at Home has touched many people's lives within its community. There are the active networks of fundraisers who work hard month after month to find the finance which the Hospice needs for its work. There are the volunteers, giving up their time to contribute to the Hospice day-care sessions. There are the nurses, at the heart of the Hospice's work, who undertake a challenging and sometimes stressful job with both professionalism and compassion. There is the smaller group, those who have managed and developed the charity, who can rightly and proudly say that, yes, West Cumbria Hospice at Home has been their achievement. And finally, there are the patients for whom West Cumbria Hospice at Home has provided the support and care to enable them to meet death in the familiar surroundings of their own homes.

West Cumbria Hospice at Home has pioneered a valuable model of hospice work, perhaps given the recognition it deserves when in 1998 the Prince of Wales agreed to become its Patron. But the organisation is not unusual in other respects: a wealth of community-based action and endeavour of all kinds is constantly being undertaken in the cities and towns of our islands. That is something to acknowledge, and to celebrate.

In the course of writing this book I asked those involved in West Cumbria Hospice at Home to share with me some of their memorable experiences, especially of people whom the Hospice had been able to help. As the book was being completed, almost as the last pages were being written, I received a fax from Eileen Palmer with one particular story. It came just in time. Here it is:

Edie was different. She'd never married, but had cared for her mum, and after her mum died she fell in love with her camera and with the mountains, and spent the rest of her life photographing the Lakeland fells.

When she knew she'd got cancer, her greatest wish was to get out in the fells again. This was a challenge as the cancer had destroyed her hip joint, making walking painfully difficult. Hospice at Home stepped in.

It was an unusual request, but a driver and a Hospice nurse were made available for the afternoon. They drove Edie out into her beloved fells, one last time. She had as much time as she needed to look, to breathe the fresh Lakeland air, to gaze at the mountains she had spent half her life photographing.

It meant everything to her. Sadly, it was the last time. She deteriorated and died, peacefully.

APPENDIX

THE NUMBER OF HOSPICE AT HOME PATIENTS EACH YEAR FROM 1987 TO MARCH 1998

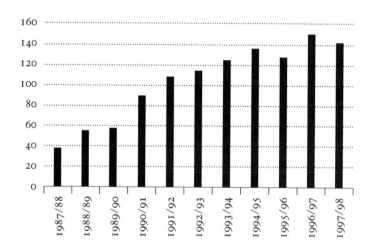

THE NUMBER OF DAYS AND NIGHTS OF CARE EACH YEAR FROM 1987 TO MARCH 1998

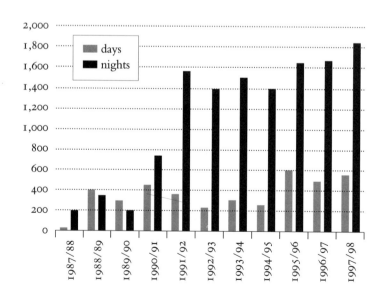

LENGTH OF EPISODES OF CARE FOR THE YEAR APRIL 1997 TO MARCH 1998

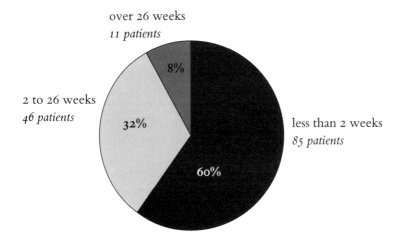

over 26 weeks
11 patients

8%

2 to 26 weeks
46 patients

32%

less than 2 weeks
85 patients

60%

Data from West Cumbria Hospice at Home 1998 annual report.

Some Useful Addresses

Association for Hospice Management
Strathcarron Hospice
Randolph Hill
Denny
Stirlingshire FK6 5HJ
Tel: 01324 826222
Fax: 01324 824576

Help the Hospices
34-44 Britannia Street
London WC1X 9JG
Tel: 0171 278 5668
Fax: 0171 278 1021
E-mail: info@helpthehospices.org.uk

Hospice Information Service
St Christopher's Hospice
51-9 Lawrie Park Road
London SE26 6DZ
Tel: 0181 778 9252
Fax: 0181 776 9345
E-mail: his@stchris.ftech.co.uk

Irish Hospice Foundation
9 Fitzwilliam Place
Dublin 2
Ireland
Tel: 00 353 1 676 5599
Fax: 00 353 1 676 5657
E-mail: info@hospice-foundation.ie

National Council for Hospice and Specialist Palliative Care Services
7th floor
1 Great Cumberland Street
London WIH 7AL
Tel: 0171 723 1639
Fax: 0171 723 5380
E-mail: enquiries@hospice-spc-council.org.uk

Natural Death Centre
20 Heber Road
London NW2 6AA
Tel: 0181 208 2853
Fax: 0181 452 6434
E-mail: rhino@dial.pipex.com
Website: www.newciv.org/worldtrans/naturaldeath.html

Scottish Partnership Agency for Palliative and Cancer Care
1a Cambridge Street
Edinburgh EHI 2DY
Tel: 0131 229 0538
Fax: 0131 228 2967

West Cumbria Hospice at Home
PO Box 5
Cockermouth
Cumbria CA13 0UP
Tel: 01900 824767

Index

PHOTOGRAPHIC CREDITS

Photographs in the book are by Ski Harrison except as follows:
Barnaby's Picture Library, London, frontispiece and page 22
AJ Potter, pages 4 and 24